The Young Old Masters
A Spiritual Guide for Young and Old

Love & Light,
Mary Norris

Living in a World of Energy

The Young Old Masters:
A Spiritual Guide for Young and Old
by
Chris Wagner, Ph.D.
Mary Norris, MSW

Living in a World of Energy

OME Press
Highland, Michigan

This book was written by Chris Wagner and Mary Norris with contributions from Brian Wagner, Meg Norris, Todd Hill, and Craig Bonacorsi.

Photos by Liz Wojnar.

Editing by Elaine Lockhart.

Cover by Linda Hazimi, Exhibited Designs, Dearborn, MI.

ISBN: 1-891876-96-1
Library of Congress Catalog Card Number: 98-91202.
Printed in the U.S.A.

Dedication Page

This book is dedicated to youth
who are the hope for our future.
Their power and wisdom
will move us all into a new age
of connection to Spirit.

With Gratitude to:

My husband, Dave.
Mary

Andy, Brian, Linda, Mary, Natalie, Pat, Patricia, Sabah, and Steve.
Chris

We are grateful to all the people in our lives who have loved us, supported us, challenged us, and been our teachers. We are not really separate – we grow together.

Table of Contents

Preface

The purpose of this book is to give you hope. Hope for you. Maybe even hope for the future of humanity.

We will introduce you to your spiritual self. You may have heard about the body / mind / spirit connection but may be uncertain what that really means in your life. We have written this book to help you **know** your spiritual self.

Spiritual experience is not something that you have to wait for. It's not something that comes only from divine intervention in a car accident with an out-of-body experience. It can come from a tranquil moment sitting beside a beautiful pond or even in the middle of a hectic day at work. It comes when the realization hits you that you are a part of everything on earth and everything on earth is a part of you. This idea sounds like some vaguely irrelevant philosophical statement when you first read it because you process it on an intellectual level. That's not good enough. You must experience the oneness of life on more than just the intellectual level. To know the spiritual self, you need to sense this oneness on an emotional, physical, and spiritual level, too.

To help move you from the understanding of the intellect to the actual experience of your spirit, this book describes our fun and games with some young adults seeking their truth. It asks you to listen to a new perspective and imagine what it would be like if this were true. We have included a playground of group and individual exercises that can help you feel and know your spiritual self.

You don't have to be "religious" in the traditional sense to be spiritual or to be aware that you have a spiritual dimension in your life. The soul is an energy force in your life, even though it is seldom talked about directly. Feelings of love, intuition, and connection are all part of the soul's energy and are a part of our own spiritual essence.

We hope to awaken, in you, the desire to explore your being, your higher self, and your connection to all life.

A Very Special Group Came Together To Explore Energy

Chris and I had a wonderful learning experience together in the summer of 1996. We had an opportunity to work with a group of young adults and teach them energy and light skills. We used the nine spiritual insights in the novel *The Celestine Prophecy*, by James Redfield, to help open spiritual awareness in the group. We discovered that the youth of today are old masters in young bodies. We want to share with you our spiritual growth experiences and bring you some of our collective wisdom about living in a world of energy.

The "Young Old Masters" who participated in our groups were ready to awaken, and we believe that many others are ready, too. People do not have to wait until they are 30, 40, or 50 years old in a life crisis to awaken to their spiritual light. Teenagers, young adults, and maybe even children are coming into the world ready to explore their body / mind / spirit connection.

We encourage you, the young, to begin your spiritual journey early. There is power and wisdom that you bring to the planet. Your parents, the Baby Boomers, may have started the revolution into expanded awareness, but you are the future of our evolution here on earth. You can lead the evolution into being a fully connected spirit in a physical body, living an aware life here on earth. It is time that we all awaken more: young and old, babies and grandparents. Awaken to the vibration of love, the energy that heals and connects all of mankind. We invite you to awaken to your higher vibration of love.

We want you to read this book and experiment with the energy exercises. If it feels right to you, use some meditation tapes to experience your spiritual energy. We found out that young people have fun exploring their souls and playing with spiritual energies. This is our hope for you, too.

Mary

Becoming Alive

We designed this book to be fun. Fun in a way that you may never yet have experienced. We had a few wild teenagers help us craft each part of it. They still know how to enjoy life in a raw, unadulterated way that adults often forget. We hope that you will feel the energy of their age as you explore, experiment and play with energy.

This book is about feeling such pleasure outside in nature, and enjoying every minute of the sun shining down on you at the beach. It is equally about enjoying every moment of that bitter winter storm that bites through your heaviest clothes as you scrape the ice off your windshield in the winter. This book is about becoming alive, about leaving behind the sleep walk most people are in, and becoming aware of yourself, your life and your purpose in being here. This book is about realizing that you are living in a world of energy and learning to sense your world. This could be the first step on your journey to higher awareness or the fiftieth. It doesn't matter because there is always more to understand and more to learn.

Once the journey down the road of self awareness is begun, it can rarely be stopped. Every single person that travels this road makes a difference. You. Yes, you. Right now. Reading this book. Are making a difference. You are caring enough to stop and take a look at your life. This is what you need to do to add spiritual energy to your life. As the ideas you learn here and elsewhere permeate who you are, you will become a beacon of... the only word that seems to fit is... "light." Blending the physical body, emotional body, mental body, and the spiritual body adds "light" to your life. This is what it means to be fully alive.

The ideas and concepts here are not about any rules or dogma or anything set-in-concrete that we all must follow. The better way to understand higher awareness involves going deep within yourself and discovering who you truly are. Have you ever thought about it at a deep level? Do you really know who you are? What you want? Do you know what you would cheerfully die for? When you know who you are, you will begin expressing that truth in your life. Perhaps the best word to apply to people following the path of self awareness is that they achieve a **clarity of self.**

This book is about achieving higher awareness, sensing energy, learning clarity of self, and having fun. It is about growing up. Not growing up like your parents did. But growing up to be a true adult, with all your power available to you, with all your awareness guiding you, with joy and fulfillment and warmth and love and health and song and connectedness and appreciation and aliveness greater than you have ever known. Use this book to take yourself to the next level on the upward spiral of creating your life.

We invite you to blend with your spirit and know the deeper love you have within.

Chris

CHAPTER 1 ❧You, Too, Are a Master

This chapter will describe for you how a group of young people, all on their own, decided that their spiritual growth was important enough to seek out teachers to help them explore. We hope that you enjoy reading about the experience they had and we encourage you to explore your own spiritual energy. Seek out the teachers, books, tools, and experiences that will assist in your learning and growth. Remember that "When the student is ready the teacher will appear." Becoming one with your spirit will bring energy, love, and light into your life.

Our Fun and Games Together

In the summer of 1996, Chris and Mary had a unique experience exploring personal energy with a group of teenagers. These young adults had gathered on their own to study the novel *The Celestine Prophecy*, by James Redfield. Redfield's words had suggested a new way to make sense out of life but they wanted help in understanding the ideas. They asked Chris and Mary to run a class for them and from that small seed has grown this book and other life-changing experiences for all of those involved.

Redfield begins his novel by talking about coincidences that help guide us in life. The meeting of Chris, Mary and the teens was such a coincidence. Mary coined the name "Young

Old Masters" to describe them. They learned quickly how to enhance their intuition, to transmit and sense energy between people, and to connect more completely with their higher guidance. Yet, there is nothing unusual about these young people. What happened to them can happen to you. Youth seem to find it easier to embrace spiritual truths than adults do.

Mary is a meditation teacher and had been facilitating spiritual growth and meditation groups with adults for 5 years. Chris is her friend who had been studying spiritual growth techniques for many years privately. They met in a meditation seminar in California in 1995 participating in a type of spiritual growth work called "Awakening Your Light Body." The seminar was run by Duane Packer and Sanaya Roman, teachers and energy workers. Though Chris and Mary lived in Michigan and studied the same Light Body work, it took a trip to California for them to meet. James Redfield would call this a "meaningful coincidence."

Although Mary had taught meditation to adults for many years, she had never really considered organizing a group of young people before. Chris had a teenage son, a new high school graduate, who along with several like-minded friends had read *The Celestine Prophecy*. This group of guys decided they wanted to learn more about "energy." Mary had a teenage daughter who was also interested in this group, so Chris and Mary decided to facilitate a class and see what happened. The coincidence began to include others.

When six, eighteen-year-old guys came in to the first meeting, all six-foot-plus tall, baggy shorts, earrings, long hair, long arms, long legs, attitudes, and egos, Mary admitted she was intimidated. Chris had warned her about the kids, but secretly she wondered what kind of spirituality could exist in this much testosterone. Mary's daughter Meg arrived wearing her "7 Year Bitch" T-shirt, red hair, black lipstick, and black fingernails. Though Chris respected Mary, he couldn't help wonder about the grunge look in the spiritual domain. They both had a lot to learn.

These young adults seemed like good people. They were joking and teasing each other as they waited for class to start. Mary and Chris sat wondering how they were going to fit in with all of this youth. Could these students who played soccer and listened to rock music really want to know about connecting to their souls? Obviously the higher powers had something in mind.

When asked, the young people already knew what they wanted to get from the class: the ability to sense energy. They had read about it or heard about it and now they wanted to experience it for themselves. Everyone decided as a group to meet for six weeks and explore the insights in *The Celestine Prophecy*. It's hard to explain in words, but in that small room in a very short period of time, spirit was present. It became clear that this was really going to work. Though many others attended the group sessions at various times throughout the class, Brian, Todd, Craig, and Meg were the main players. These four were not only ready to play with energy but were also willing to assist in the creation of this book.

Before working with this group of young people, Mary didn't realize just how closed down most adults really were. When the energy of these kids started to flow, it was like turning up the volume on the speakers and having the whole room shake. To have the energy of youth combined with the wisdom of the Masters in these young bodies created some powerful group energies. For Chris, having spent many hard years trying to learn about spiritual truths coming from a background as a computer engineer, the way these young people picked up new skills was almost depressing and definitely amazing. It was so easy for them. They didn't have to suffer like adults to learn. It was like the difference between jumping in the sea of energy with your whole body rather than sticking in one toe at a time. Youths jump; adults test the water. Neither path is right or wrong, but making the jump sure looks fun from the perspective of a toe-at-a-time-er.

As the classes began to unfold, some things became very clear. When the young people were asked to focus on spiritual energy, the energy in the room increased. There was a flow moving through our conversations. One idea lead to another higher idea. It was as if some great guide was dropping bits of energy into the room to be absorbed by all. No other parents were present, so the group members could be as free and honest about their energy experiences as they wished. Talking about "guides" and "spirits" and "sensing energy" seemed natural. Their awakening had begun, and it was fast and easy. The coincidence of the group coming together created a way, a flow, in which all could learn from each other.

It seemed like God, or the higher energies, or our spirits had brought just the right group together. There was a synergy in the group, a blending of the energies that made sense. Like a beautiful collage, if you looked at any individual part, it could seem odd and out of place, but when placed in the context of the other pieces, it seemed a perfect part of a beautiful whole. You could just feel the expectations in the students, waiting to, at long last, explore the spiritual self they knew they had. It felt like Mary and Chris could have done or said anything and each individual would still have found the way to their own awakening.

When you gather together as a group, a special force begins to move among the group members. This happens especially when you explore spiritual insights together. As the conversations moved around the circle of young masters, the energy in the room began to lighten and expand as if the group had the ability to learn and know more. It was clear that this group was meant to explore energy together.

The Players

This book has been a group effort. We want you to meet everyone involved, the "players." When a group gathers to study spiritual truths, the students become the teachers and the teachers become the students as all participants learn from each other. We certainly heard the wisdom of the masters being spoken through these young adults and include their words here.

Brian

My name is Brian Wagner. I'm 18 years old and am a first year student at Michigan State University. I play soccer and the piano and like alternative music.

One of the biggest issues in my life, long before I started actually pursuing spirituality, has been my purpose. I can remember as a kid lying in bed practicing counting to 100 and wondering how all the adults I saw could be content with their lives. I figured there was no way that simply growing up, going to school, going to college, getting a job, getting married, and then having kids was all that there was to life. Eventually, I kind of gave up looking for the answer. I attributed my lack of understanding to my immaturity. I decided that I would find the answer later in life. All I had to do was wait.

Well, call me impatient, but I'm 18 now and I realize that if it hasn't come yet, it's not going to. Even though I don't have the experience that my elders do, I do have as much wisdom as they do. I realize, now, that I have to decide what my purpose is. Without knowing my purpose, it's not clear how I can be content with the typical life that people live today. Finding my purpose is one of the most important things that has led me into exploring myself and my spirituality.

The most profound experience I had before we started *The Celestine Prophecy* class was when Todd, my brother Andy, my dad, and I took a tour of Europe and traveled into Switzerland. Switzerland was one of the only stops on our tour that wasn't a total tourist trap. We stayed in a real Swiss hotel and had very few people who spoke English to help us out.

On one of the days of our stay there, after lunch, Todd, Andy, Carla, and Guy (two people we had met on the tour) went out for a walk. Instead of being social like I normally would, I walked way ahead of everyone leading them wherever I felt like going. Eventually, we wandered over to the side of a large field to watch some people playing soccer. I noticed a smaller field on cement with smaller goals and people our age (16 at the time) playing on it. We asked them if we could play and they accepted.

The four of us (without Carla) took on the six of them (they had subs). Andy and Guy had little experience with soccer and were smaller and younger than most of their team, so we really had a challenge ahead of us. To make a long story short, we all played the best soccer we had ever played, winning 21-18. I personally amazed myself by shooting almost hard enough to knock them down and by perfectly putting in the three last goals (we had been tied 18-18). The connection and passing between myself and Todd on the field that day was absolutely amazing. We knew exactly what the other was going to do. After we won, I felt happier than I had ever felt before. That was my best energy experience before the class.

The most exciting thing about this work for me is the application to my everyday life. The best example of this to me is the way fights and arguments go. I can see people using energy-stealing techniques and defense techniques. When I am in a high-energy state, I can see exactly where the people are coming from and a few ways to solve their problems. I also like how well I can sense the way people are truly feeling even when they say otherwise. I feel as though this work continuously helps me to treat people the way I want to, act the way I want to, deal with my life better, and just be who I truly am.

Craig

Hello, my name is Craig Bonacorsi. I am 18 years old. I am a Music Theater Performance major at Western Michigan University. At the age of ten I moved to Hartland, Michigan. One of the first people I met was Todd Hill. We have remained friends since and it is through him that I was able to gain a whole new outlook on life.

It amazes me how easy it is to ignore my intuitions and write things off as a coincidence. The things that we have done as a group and the things that I have experienced have made wonderful differences in my perception of everything around me. To me, it is much easier to believe in things when I have examples from my life to support them. I can think of one major example of my awakening. In the group, the idea of telling the others about something that we had viewed as a coincidence came into discussion. When my turn to speak came around, I almost felt embarrassed to talk. It didn't seem like I had any thought-bending "coincidences" to speak of. I just picked a small thing and started talking. My words went something like this:

I haven't experienced any major coincidences in my life. So, I'm just going to talk about some little things. It all started about my sophomore year. I had a lot of extra time on my hands and it just so happened that a good friend of mine was the backstage manager for the high school drama club. He needed extra help so I volunteered. I loved being around the people, and working on the show, but I could hardly stand to be backstage, not being seen by the audience. I wanted just the opposite. Sure enough, I auditioned for the next show the high school had. I got cast in a couple of bit parts. I showed up at every rehearsal and made sure I knew all of my lines. When it came time to perform I knew I wanted to be center stage, in the spotlight. That fall, I made plans to go to Cedar Point with a friend of mine who was going to go audition for a community theater show. This show was a musical, involving singing. I had restricted my singing to my basement, and had never sung in front of anyone before. Somehow, he managed to talk me into auditioning. I was terrified, but I sang anyway. Much to my surprise, we returned to Cedar Point to find that I had a solo. This show came to be one of the best experiences of my life.

Over the course of the next few months, I did two more high school shows. One night as I was in my friend Dan's room. I was looking through a pile of papers and I noticed an interesting photograph. I asked him about it and he told me that it was from a summer institute that he had gone to. Two days later I was called to the counseling office. I was surprised when they gave me a photocopied packet on the very institute that my friend and I had just spoke about. I read the information and found one section that really caught my attention. It was titled "Music Theatre Performance." At this point in time I had toyed around with the idea of acting for a living, but never really took it seriously. This institute was at Western Michigan University, and I just knew that this was what I wanted to do for the rest of my life. The only problem was I had to be accepted into the program. Attending the Institute involved an audition in acting, singing, and dance. One month later I received my letter of acceptance.

So, between having a friend on the backstage crew, being dragged into an audition, and finding a picture, I had been influenced all the way. Over the course of the past few years I have been directed along a path towards what I am doing today. Every time I have wandered off of the path, I have been bumped back on by a coincidence. Coincidences have completely shifted my life into what it is now.

When I stopped speaking, everyone in the room was staring at me with grins on their faces. Then Mary asked me to repeat my first and last statements. I thought about it for a minute and spoke. I said, "I haven't had any major coincidences in my life, and coincidences have completely shifted my life into what it is now." Suddenly everything became much clearer to me. It was so easy to write off some major things as simple coincidences. Since then I have seen so many things that would have slipped by me before.

Being a Music Theatre Performance major, I have a lot of stress and doubts about my future. The things I have learned from this group have helped me more than I ever would have expected. Using meditation and techniques that I have learned has made my auditions and performances much less difficult and stressful. The thing that I enjoyed most is that for the first time ever there is no force to believe in anything. The things presented are set out as an experience, not rock-hard fact. There is no religious or scientific connection. It may be that not every person gets the same experiences. Everybody gets out of it what is right for them. It was made very clear to me that I could either believe or not believe. The class was an opportunity to be exposed to something amazing and I was given the freedom to make out of it what I chose. To me that choice was the most important thing behind everything here.

Meg

I believe Todd, Craig, Brian, and I have been spiritual Masters our whole lives. By the way, I am 16 years old, have red hair and blue eyes and go to Dearborn High School in Michigan. I now know for a fact we were all brought together by a higher force. The boys and I, at least from my perspective, are one entity of light and energy. If one is missing from a meditation, my being, the soul part of myself, feels a little incomplete. It's not that my right frequency of energy goes away, but it can be made stronger each time all of us meet together. I am the only female in the group and the youngest. One thing I noticed immediately is that I felt no isolation whatsoever. I felt connected. It might be the fact that they are more mature than the boys I am used to encountering, but I believe that we can all speak on the same energy level and therefore can relate to each other. I've learned to take my inner energy and reflect it outward to better my life. I have been high on this positive energy we generate together many times. At times it is so strong, people experience it with me. For example, a certain friend I have is usually bitter and argues with me more than once a week. I learned that I could direct the energy I create from a meditation to make him happier. It also made my energy stronger knowing I'd made another person happier.

I like how I am since I've taken these classes. No one really realizes that we are all spirits connected through our energy. I now know more about people in general and how all our spirits interact with each other.

Todd

I am 18 years old and a student at Michigan State University. I am majoring in Psychology and Computer Engineering. I first began to look at spirituality in my life last summer as a member of a small class on *The Celestine Prophecy*. At that point I had no idea what I was looking for out of my life, but I was sure that there must be more than what I was living. I found myself frustrated and preoccupied with the minor details of my life. I had had many intense experiences that made me feel euphoric or overcome with joy, but only for a short period of time, I had no idea how to hold on to the feeling. I found myself yearning for intense experiences and disappointed with the mundane-ness of my everyday life.

Spirituality, for me, is a continuing awakening to the underlying and ever-present energy surrounding all living things. This energy gives me such a peaceful feeling when I take the time to be aware of it. I can remember back to specific times in my life when I was aware of this energy, it filled me with an intense feeling of clarity and being. I can remember sitting in an observation deck high in the Swiss Alps looking out over the clouds and the mountains, feeling so energized about my life. I felt so tranquil and at peace and I remember thinking how perfect life can be sometimes. I felt so connected to my surroundings, I never wanted to leave.

I find that when I can connect with the feeling I had on the mountain top, life seems to be so much simpler and I just know what I am supposed to do. Spirituality has provided a way for me to connect to this feeling of purpose and has brought me much insight and direction in my life. When I am faced with a situation or feeling that I don't understand, I find it amazing how I can just simply meditate or go for a walk in the woods and be struck by insight that makes the situation clear. I look at this as my soul or higher self enlightening me to what I already know. I believe everyone has the ability to do this if they truly look within themselves for the truth. I have gained much confidence in myself and my decisions because of my ability to determine what is right for me in any challenge life presents.

For me, spirituality has not been some great quest or lifestyle change, rather it has given me the strength and confidence to follow my own truth regardless of outside influences. Spirituality has provided me with many tools for looking at the energy and truth in situations. This has left me feeling that I am empowered in these situations rather than just doing what somebody else wants or doing what I had always done before. The most important part for me in my spiritual growth is my ever-increasing ability to look at what's right for me in any given situation and thus learn more about who I truly am.

Chris

My name is Christian Wagner, though no one has called me that since my grandmother died long ago; I've grown used to the name Chris. I'm a college professor in the department of computer science and engineering at a state-supported university in Michigan but I'm probably the oddest professor there since my Ph.D. is in educational psychology. That was because I wanted to understand the human mind and find ways to construct human-like intelligence inside of a computer.

I would like to tell you just two things. The intensity of life never disappears. You can feel the loves and fears of life as well after the age of 40 as you can before the age of 20.

Also, the path of spiritual awakening is available to anyone, no matter what your background or beliefs.

I certainly didn't start my life by taking an energetic view of our human existence. I was a regular guy, doing his job, raising his kids, married to the same woman for 18 years, loyal, faithful, an all around nice guy. I felt good about myself, I thought. But then I started having personal problems. I was feeling victimized. People in my life were doing bad things to me. And this after I had been such a stand-up guy. Life wasn't fair. It wasn't right. I'd been good, where were the rewards?

One of the hardest decisions I ever made was to go into therapy. Maybe it's harder for a man than a woman, maybe not. But I had to face it squarely that my life was not functioning at all well. I made emergency phone calls to friends, I needed help, right away. I wanted to find the truth of the situation. I had to know - was I nuts or what?

I found a name. I went to my first therapy session, and didn't even understand what the therapist tried to tell me. She asked me why someone had to be right and someone had to be wrong? Why couldn't it be true that we all live in different worlds with different views, all correct? I didn't get it! As she listened, she guided. Patiently. Without a lot of comment. I left the office with an appointment for the next week. When I got to my car, I couldn't drive because of the tears streaming down my face. I sobbed and wailed for maybe twenty minutes. Such a relief. A long held emotional closure had started to open. And I did not feel judged.

That was many years ago now. I have worked on myself every day since then. I went to therapy for a time. I've read a hundred books and browsed thousands. I've attended seminars and taught others. I keep a journal. I still do the same job, but better. I have the same children, but treat them so much better. I divorced, but it the right thing to do. One thing that is very clear about the difference between the old me and the new me: **now I am alive and aware**.

What have I learned from all of this, sometimes painful, experience?

Life is about me listening to my heart about the real experiences I have and guiding my footsteps by reference to actual events in *my* life. That is where I found God, sitting with me in every moment of every day. That's a rather invigorating perspective.

The world is changing in a way that fills me with hope. Hope. An expectation that something good may actually happen to me. Sometimes, it may seem that the world is falling apart, with problems too great for any of us to solve. But that is only one view of the world. Just as reasonable a view is that the world has never been in a better place to integrate our diverse abilities and knowledge into a global solution to worldwide problems. If we can get each individual person to do their small part, to listen to divine wisdom, the massed effect of our combined wills could do anything.

You can make your life better, appreciably better, by practicing the ideas presented here. Surprisingly, the ideas are simple and straightforward. The problem has been that no one seems to tell people how to view the world differently while they are young. So we all tend to grow up with problems similar to those experienced by people thousands of years ago. Enough already. Let this coming generation be the first one that is more enlightened.

Finally, though it is rare for someone to be able to eliminate all strife from their life, you can move now to make your life rich beyond anything you have imagined.

My life is so full now, so rich, so textured. Mary and I met at a meditation conference in California and have been working together ever since. As we have taken a healthy, truly adult, understanding of life and taught it to young adults, we have found them so totally receptive and so totally in agreement. They seem to immediately see that truth is a better way to live their lives and see their worlds.

Enjoy the book to the fullest. Always keep learning. And remember that emotion is energy flow. It is always changing. Painful emotions are not permanent as long as you open them up to the light of day. Although we all make mistakes and slip back from our best, it is in our best interests to consciously take the choice that moves us closer to our highest good. It is now time for people to grab their spirituality and own it. Not just the clergy, the religious people, the hippies, or the new-agers, but all of us ordinary folk must reconnect with God.

Mary

I am Mary, a medical social worker and a spiritual teacher. I have been teaching a particular form of meditation called "Awakening Your Light Body" for five years. I have also been teaching Celestine Prophecy Insights groups for two years. I am a wife and the mother of a 20-year-old son and 16-year-old Meg.

When I thought about what I really wanted to share with you and thought about what I have learned exploring my spiritual self, I became somewhat overwhelmed. I have learned so much in the last seven years and I continue to learn spiritually every day. I have learned to let go of other people's energy, I have learned to respect myself, I have learned to pay attention to my intuition and higher guidance, I have learned to accept and love myself and because of this I can accept and love others more deeply. I am in the process of becoming the kind of teacher and leader I always wanted to be: a person who leads from the heart and knows there is a power greater than the personality self.

I have teachers and a spiritual support group who inspire me to live my highest potential. My teachers, Duane Packer and Sanaya Roman (who channel the energies DaBen and Orin), offer live seminars in Oregon each year. Many of their students, who are also teachers, come from around the world to participate in this work together. These events allow all of us to practice some advanced energy and light skills that help us more fully know our souls. That in itself is a great event, but the fun for me is beyond what I learn from my teachers. The most interesting and exciting part of these live seminars is joining together with about 300 other people in a large ballroom and actually coming together as one energy. It is amazing!

Imagine, together as a group, all these people of like mind, becoming one huge vibration of positive energy. When I am in these groups, I am certain I can do anything in life. I rise out of my fears and doubts in life and see the world as a loving planet full of energy. I even rise out of my body, connect with my soul, and bring some of that energy back into my body. I know this sounds crazy because it even sounds crazy to me as I write it. But I have **experienced it** so I can't lie to myself about the beauty and wonder of exploring my soul. When we join together like this we all become greater beings of light. If you really want to have fun living your life, come together with 300 of your friends, vibrate at the spiritual level and talk to your souls; it's a great experience.

All the great individuals who are working on themselves to grow spiritually and vibrationally are helping to change planet earth. When all the great souls of you Young Old Masters awaken it will be like creating a world rock concert of positive light. I wonder if that is the real meaning of "Rock and Roll," that we will all learn to rock (vibrate) together and have peace and love roll over the earth.

I know now that I am a part of the evolution of the planet, and if you are reading this book, you are too.

Growing spiritually is fun.

The Young Old Masters

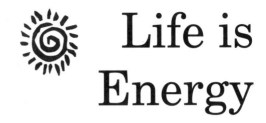

CHAPTER 2 · Life is Energy

One of the hardest things to do in life is to change the way you look at things, to have a different perspective on what your life is about. We spoke to the young people about viewing themselves as vibrations of energy in a world of energy. We provided experiences that helped them feel the truth of their own energy. The experiences they had were unique and different for each individual. As you explore your own energy, earth energy, life energy, your world view can change in a way just perfect for you. In the following chapters we want you to read about our group experiences, to understand some energetic principles, and to experience your own energy by trying some of the exercises at the end of each chapter.

Our Fun and Games Together

We began our groups by asking the members to focus on their soul. We ask you, the reader, to do the same. **We want you to know that you are a great spiritual being.** Just imagine for a moment that you are a powerful being of energy and light. Imagine that your physical body is only one part of who you are. The spiritual part is really the captain of your energy ship. You might imagine that the body, emotions, mind, and soul are the whole of who you are, floating about in the sea of your life. But it is the soul, the higher self, the part of yourself that is most closely connected to God's energy, that navigates and directs your ship.

In the movie *Powder*, the main character's mother gets hit by lightning just before he is born. The lightning strike awakens abilities in this young man to sense energy. He has the power to heal others, has higher intelligence, and has increased psychic abilities. We do not have to be hit by lightning to awaken our own energy abilities (although sometimes it feels that way). All people on earth are a body, emotions, a mind, and a spirit. When we become more acquainted with the spirit part, we have access to our own higher energy senses.

How do you learn about the spirit self? How do you feel the energy for yourself? Higher energy can be sensed, learned from, and absorbed so that you live your highest potential. But how do you experience or "see" this for yourself? Learning how to connect to your soul part is just like connecting to a great rock song. There is a rhythm, an energy, a beat that calls to you and changes your inner vibration as you listen. Often, the poetry in the lyrics can speak to your heart when you connect with the truths the words portray. The beat can speak to your physical body and call you to move to that vibration. This is connecting with the energy. The music and words are not separate from your body. When experienced, the rock song becomes a part of who you are and changes you energetically. This is what happens when you connect with your soul.

Like connecting to the music, you can learn to sense your own inner energy and the energy of other people. You can learn how to focus your awareness and expand your consciousness. You can also learn to release negative energy from your life so you are not a part of others' negativity and problems. You, too, can experience the wisdom of your soul and create a life that flows.

The higher energies are available to anyone. You can learn some techniques for accessing your higher self and expanding your awareness. Many young people have the ability to sense spiritual energies and have some profound energy experiences. This book has been written to help you explore and experience all the parts of your energy. We want to share with you our group experience and also share our vision for many groups of teens and young adults gathering around the country, exploring and experiencing a spiritual awakening. We ask you to take on a new perspective, viewing your life as energy.

Listen and Imagine

Living in a Higher Spiritual Flow

We want you to learn how to connect more clearly with your higher self. Learning about your spiritual self is fun and can awaken your highest potential. Our higher self accepts us just the way we are. You will never be told by your higher self that your hair is too long, your clothes are grungy, your attitudes are unacceptable, and you will never amount to anything. Your soul is constantly shining the light of love on you and our goal is to have you experience that for yourself.

We are complex beings of energy and light. We are affected by the other energies around us. You can learn how to gain control over how other people's energy affects you. At your core you are a loving being. Part of your growth and learning will be to remember or re-learn about your own loving nature. You can also learn how to transmit love and evolve your relationships with others to a higher level of energy exchanges. We believe you are a powerful source of love and light for the world. We want you to believe this too.

Remember the young are masterful souls. Becoming aware of your mastery at a young age enriches your life. What if you could go within, as a master does, and sense what is right for you? There are many choices you will have to make, such as, jobs, colleges, relationships, and careers. What if you could "sense" more clearly what the highest choice is for you? Our intention is to have you learn and make choices from a space of Mastery rather than a space of fear. We are all evolving out of an age of pain and suffering and into an age of creating with love and joy. We want you to be able to create with joy.

There are moments in your life when we are already living in a higher flow. It may be happening when you play your perfect soccer game, create your perfect artistic expression, or gather with friends at the coffee house for conversation. The "higher flow" is a moment when somehow everything seems to be going perfectly and everything you do works. As you learn how to increase your spiritual connection in life, you will have more perfect moments in time. As the body, mind, emotions, and spirit are aligned, you will express your true personal power. Deepak Chopra calls this playing in your field of pure potential energy. Your spiritual essence is pure potential energy waiting to help you create your own higher flow.

We want you to have a better life. A better life than your parents and grandparents. This is not the same as just having a better life because you have more material things; rather, having a life of joy because you are living your highest potential. Working with the exercises and meditations in this book will assist you in gaining a greater understanding of your life on the energy level. You can choose to live in higher rather than lower energies. Connecting with your higher self and learning how masterful you are can be like taking a moonlight walk on a warm sandy beach with the person you love. At that moment in time you know you are living in a higher flow.

Experiencing Energy

This book is about experience. Having things happen to you. We want this book to be an experience for you. Every moment you spend in life is an opportunity to learn, to grow, to improve, and to be happy. Consider the possibility of allowing this book to turn into such an event for you.

Read each chapter, experiment with the energy exercises at the end of the chapter and listen to a meditation tape of your choice. (We have developed, and will soon have available for distribution, a set of our own meditation tapes specifically created to complement the chapters.) All this can be done alone or with a group of friends. Take your time exploring the concepts presented within. Sensing the energy of the soul often comes in quiet moments of contemplation when you take the time to find your own answers. Repeating something you do not truly understand will help you learn about the depths of your soul as the answers are revealed to you. Learning energy skills happens gradually as you practice and develop higher awareness.

Meditation tapes are created to help us reach expanded states of consciousness. States that are beyond just thinking.

Some people call these states "soul spaces" that can help you feel more peaceful and connected to your higher self. All people will have different experiences during a guided meditation or musical journey. Allow your experience to be right for you. There are no right or wrong ways to experiences higher states of consciousness.

The more you practice and play with meditation, the more profound your experiences will be. We have also found that energy experiences will usually be stronger in a group rather than alone.

Spiritual growth work asks you to question much of what society says you should believe in. It does not tell you the answers, but asks instead that you investigate a way by which the highest part of your being can guide you to the truth.

Experiencing Group Energies

Group energy makes a big difference. As powerful as the techniques and perspectives provided here are when you read them in the book, the ability to know and process the information is greatly enhanced when shared with a group of friends. A great way to work with this material is to gather together some friends, decide on a place and time to meet, and make a commitment to read and experience the material together. Coming together once a week seems to work well. We have some exercises for you to experiment with later in this chapter in a section called "The Playground."

Do the energy exercises and taped meditations together. Discuss how each of you experience the processes, remembering that there is no right or wrong way to experience any of this. Respect the individuality of all the members by creating an environment of acceptance. When doing work that asks you to be open and honest about yourself and your deepest thoughts and feelings, you are asking something that can be scary for some people. We suggest the following ground rules:

- Whatever comes up in the group is considered confidential.
- Nothing personal will be repeated outside of the group.
- We are all really the same and need to be accepted for who we are.
- No fair laughing at people's stupid comments.

Most of these experiences will be fun and light. Occasionally there will be sadness or seriousness uncovered in the group. Use common sense. **If one of the members has a serious problem, we recommend they seek professional advice.** It is not the responsibility of the group to handle serious problems. Be friends and supporters of each other in your growth. You may discover, as we did, that you all have a deep spiritual connection to each other.

Respecting Religions

This book is about spiritual energies and spiritual flow. There is spiritual energy and flow in every religion. There is also spiritual energy and spiritual flow that exists outside of the form of religion. All religions work on assisting people with their spiritual needs. When exploring spiritual energies, some people feel it is threatening to their religious beliefs, but we are here to say you can have both. You can have strong religious beliefs and explore spiritual energy, too. We do not suggest that anyone change their religion because they are exploring spiritual truths and higher energies. We want you to learn and grow and love each other and love yourself and evolve into a great human being. That is what the Young Old Masters is all about: experiencing your greatness. Most religions want that for you, too.

The Playground

Since this is the first time you've been on our playground, we'd like to explain some of the equipment to you. First, we have a field of questions for you to **"Adventure and Explore."** Then, we have a place for you to **"Create and Play"** with experiencing energy and creating your own higher flow. Finally, we move into a guided meditation to help you **"Touch and Sense"** your higher self.

Adventure and Explore

The rules of this game are simple. You just have to honestly say who you are with respect to certain ideas or questions. There are no right or wrong answers; you don't even have to give one if you feel uncomfortable. Each person simply explores and expresses their own truth, either aloud or to themselves.

Let the game on the merry-go-round begin.

Round 1: Have you ever had the feeling of deja vue? Have you ever had an extraordinary coincidence?

Round 2: Have you ever had a strong intuition that proved to be true? Have you ever known what another person is thinking?

Round 3: Have you ever experienced anything that you feel is outside of all scientific explanation? If you can think of even one thing, what does that tell you about science?

Round 4: Do you believe in angels or spirits? Why?

Round 5: Have you ever found yourself saved miraculously from certain disaster by some force outside of yourself?

Round 6: Do you believe you have a soul? What do you think happens to you when you die?

Round 7: What are your spiritual or religious beliefs? Do you believe in God? Do your beliefs bother you?

Round 8: What is your single, best story about yourself that you would like to share with the group?

Round 9: Tell the group about a high energy experience that you have had. A time when you can remember when things were flowing and happening easily for you.

Round 10: When you know you are energetically low, what usually happens to you? What kind of mood are you in? How do you communicate with others? What can you do to get out of this low mood?

Round 11: When you know you are energetically high, what usually happens to you? What kind of mood are you in? How do you communicate with others? How long do you stay in this high state?

Create and Play

In this section we have developed some energy exercises for you to try. Feel free to add your own creative ideas or leave out any part that does not make sense for you or your group. Since this is the first set of exercises, we would like you to practice shifting the energy in yourself, the room, and throughout the group.

Creating a Quiet Sacred Space.

1. Choose someone to be the leader to take you through this exercise. If you are doing this exercise alone, imagine that a group of souls is joining you to go through the experience with you.

2. Have everyone in the group sit comfortably in a circle. Turn down the light, put on some quiet background music or a meditation music tape, place a candle in the middle of the circle, light the candle, and have everyone get quiet, turning their focus toward creating peace in the room.

3. After everyone is quiet, comfortable and peaceful, the group leader will read the following **very slowly** and quietly. This should take about 15 minutes.

Let us begin this evening by staring into the flame and focusing on the light of the candle. As you stare allow your body to relax, your breathing to get quieter and let go of any thoughts at this time. Imagine for a moment that as you stare at the candle you can see a gentle glow of energy or light coming off of the flame. With your imagination allow the energy of the flame to extend out through the room and flow through your physical body. Take your time and pretend that this energy from the candle is filling you with light. (Pause.)

Allow yourself to get quieter and more peaceful and imagine now that you are filled with a quiet gentle light. Breath in the light deeply, and close your eyes. As you close your eyes and relax even more, imagine that you can feel a cocoon of light all around you and you are beginning to sense the energy of your higher self. (Pause.)

As you move out into this cocoon of light, you begin to sense the energy of the others in the room. You may imagine them as light, or feel them as a subtle vibration or experience them as colors or patterns of light. Imagine that as a group you are becoming one large sphere of light and your energy is getting brighter and expanding even more. (Pause.)

The light of your group and your cocoon has called in the spirit of a great teacher. Imagine for a moment that you can sense the energy presence of a great spirit or angel and that this being has come to join your group and share its love with you. And now without questioning, imagine that you are opening your cocoon to receive the love being transmitted by this teacher. (Pause.)

Even if it feels like you are making it up, imagine that you can feel or sense the loving vibration being sent to you at this time. Allow this loving light to flow into your physical body and sense how you are feeling now. (Pause.)

The great teacher smiles at you and your group and bids you farewell for now. Sit quietly for a few moments remembering your experience. There is great love and light available to you from the universe. (Pause.)

Imagine now that you are coming back into present time and reality. You are becoming more alert and awake. When you are ready, in your own time, come back completely and open your eyes, returning to the room and your group.

4.   Take some time to sit quietly and sense the shift in energy that you created.

5.   Discuss your experiences, observing the differences and similarities. Remember that some people may not wish to share and that is fine.

Touch and Sense

In this section, we encourage you to play with meditation. Meditation is not a religious statement about anything. It is a physiological state that is well understood and accessible to anyone. When in a meditative state, you can find the truth about where you are and what you are doing. Sometimes the truth can be painful, and sometimes beautiful.

Meditation can be done in silence, but we have found that for people new to meditation, having music in the background makes it easier. Also, meditations can have a specific focus on an issue important to you, such as using quiet time to visualize good health, improved relationships, or any positive outcome.

Participating in a meditation is allowing yourself to explore your inner world. Some people are able to experience color, light, images, or physical sensations through meditation. But know that on any given day for any particular person, you may feel nothing, or your mind might be filled with the day's chatter. Don't worry about that, just let today's meditation be what it is. Tomorrow's will be different.

Guided meditations are meant to help you to relax, experience being with your own internal energies, and have fun. If you do not enjoy meditating or don't want to meditate, then don't. Just listening to tapes without trying to meditate will give you much benefit.

It is now time to listen to a guided meditation journey. Get yourself in a comfortable physical position, sitting or lying down in a quiet room. Be ready to play a tape in its entirety, which takes about 30 minutes. Try to find a time and space when you will not be interrupted. Turn off the phone and the pagers. Some people light a candle to help them prepare a quiet inner space.

The Young Old Masters

3 # Your Energy

To help you connect to your higher self, the first thing you need to do is to become aware that you are energy and energy is everywhere around you. It is easy to understand that electricity is energy because that's what you've always been taught. It is harder to believe that you are energy: energies of intellect, emotion, body, and spirit. Your energy can flow, radiate, and glow in some ways very similar to an electrical current. This chapter gives you an understanding of these ideas as well as some exercises that will make you feel the energy for yourself. When you do begin to know yourself as energy, your spiritual growth and your knowledge of the higher energies accelerates.

Our Fun and Games Together

As the group gathered on a Tuesday evening, it was clear that these young people had a lot of energy. It was a small room and with six young men, one young woman and two teachers, we were close. After introductions we asked them to ponder the question: "What do you want to learn about your spiritual self?" The answers were somewhat surprising, but the common thought was that each wanted to learn more about their higher self. Todd said he wanted to learn how to channel. (Channeling is connecting with a guide or your higher self and bringing through the higher energy or spiritual wisdom.) Meg said she wanted to be more intuitive and Brian wanted to feel and experience higher energies. One group member really surprised us when he said he thought this may be his last incarnation. He knew about reincarnation and felt that he might grow to enlightenment in this lifetime. We, as teachers, were amazed. Where did these kids come from?

We began by discussing *The Celestine Prophecy* and coincidences that are leading us in life. What is that force that has just the right person cross your path? A person who may become your best friend, a person who may share your life experiences with you or an acquaintance that says just the right thing to lead you toward your higher good. We asked the groups members to keep track of the coincidences in their life, the subtle messages they get daily, or maybe even a déjà vu. We pointed out that your higher self helps you pay attention to messages by the subtle feelings you get.

We suggested to the group that we know by our feelings if something is right for us. We asked these kids if they had ever done anything they just knew wasn't right? Not just because their parents didn't want them to do it, but because they got this feeling in their gut that it just wasn't right. The whole group laughed and looked around with knowing smiles. Yes, they knew that feeling well. Everyone had done something contrary to what they were feeling and then had been sorry later.

Even though it is hard to believe, this is a friendly universe that wants to help us in life. As a being of energy that is a body, emotions, mind and spirit, we are constantly interacting with the energy of the universe. Quite often, it is the feeling part of us that warns of danger or leads us to joy. It is the physical body that gives us the messages through these physical feelings. We can learn much about ourselves, by observing our emotions and the sensations in our physical body. It is part of our sensing system. We pointed out to the group that we don't have to touch someone to sense when a friend is angry. We pick up negative vibes from a distance. This is part of our higher intelligence, our ability to feel.

It is our mind and our thoughts that give us new ideas and creative solutions for life. Our higher self is like a tour guide when you are in a foreign country, it will send you higher thoughts when you need guidance. But it helps to learn and observe the difference between our higher and lower thoughts. The spirit is gently guiding us onto our higher path by sending coincidences our way. When we looked at our group coincidence, it seemed like all our souls consulted together and said, "Hey we better send these young people to those teachers because they have much to learn from each other." And, so here we all sit in Mary's healing center exploring energy. Somehow we all heard the message from our higher selves.

There is energy in thoughts, there is energy in emotions, there is energy in our lives. It is here to bring us into a higher awareness. In our group, that first night, there was the energy of excitement, an energy that said a great coincidence has taken place and Chris and Mary could sense it. We are not our bodies. We are not our thoughts. We are not our emotions. We are not just our spirits. In this life, we are the interacting energies of all of these parts. As we concluded our discussion for the evening and experienced a guided meditation together, we opened our hearts and connected energetically. We could sense each other as beings and we could also sense our higher selves. The feeling was pure joy, and we knew in our guts this was right.

Listen and Imagine

Everything is Energy

All of our physical world and all of our physical self is made up of energy. Cells, molecules, and atoms move and interact in certain ways to create all the different patterns that eventually become a house, a garden, or a newborn baby; all vibrating at different frequencies and putting out their own distinct energy. Our body is an energy system, our emotions are an energy system, our mind is an energy system, and our spirit is an energy system. We want you to begin to learn and sense the different energies of who you are. Why? Because you can improve your life by adding spiritual light to any or all of your systems. When "hands-on healers" focus their minds and harness the spiritual energy flowing through their own body, they can then transmit this energy to another person as long as that person is receptive. They do this by learning about their own energy flows, by practicing sensing energy, and by connecting with the higher flow. In our groups we discussed the four energy systems and practiced increasing our energy awareness. This is not magic. By becoming more aware and believing in yourself, all people can learn about energy flows.

Physical Energies

A new CD plays in the background; Enigma 3. The music pulses and a human voice with a wonderfully sharp edge to it sings a melody. Other background voices and sounds weave counterpoint melodies and rhythms around it. A light but insistent drum beat comes through and the beat is unavoidable. It is early in the morning and winter has left almost a foot of new-fallen snow on the ground. Near blizzard conditions with strong winds whip up the top layer of snow, swirling it with yet more snow, making it almost impossible to go out.

The warmth in the room stands in stark contrast to what is only a window pane of glass away. A warm cup of fresh hazelnut coffee wafts its pleasant aromas to the nose: the nutty and bitter taste of the coffee awakens and warms. We have the ability to sense our world physically, and the body gives us messages all the time.

But let's face it, we have a love/hate relationship with our physical bodies. We think we are too fat, too thin, ugly, unfit, and sometimes even feel as if we are in the wrong body. In fact, our constant inner criticism of the body often has us ignore the messages we get. Our body tells us it is tired, but we won't lie down; it is hungry but we won't eat; it is full, but we keep eating anyway; it is stressed but we won't take the pressure off. Is it any wonder that we have a lot of stress-related illnesses in our world? That is because we do not listen to our bodies.

What if we think of our body as a fine-tuned energy system, (which it is), and begin to pay attention to what we are sensing energetically. It is kind of comical to think that we are obsessed with the physical body in one way (Hollywood), but we won't pay attention to our own natural signals. It really is amazing to simply look at the five senses and quickly you begin to see we are a dynamic sensing system in action and reaction.

We have five senses that help us know our three-dimensional world: sight, hearing, taste, smell, and touch. Each of these senses sends energy signals to us when some aspect of our physical world meets and impinges on the boundary of our body. All the senses are important, but touch seems so central to our feeling good.

Touch, the sense that lets us truly "feel" ourselves and another human being. Touching other people is very important to our well-being and connectedness. Feeling "warm" comes largely from the sense of touch. Making love is primarily a connection with another through the sense of touch. We can even learn how to "touch" and be "touched" by the spiritual energies.

Respecting our five senses and the messages we are receiving is part of becoming a more energetically aware being. Nearly everyone enjoys a magnificent sunset or sunrise, seeing the bright colors through the clouds and the sky as the sun leaves or arrives. The sounds of ocean waves breaking on the seashore seems universally to soothe the spirit. Rock music, country music, classical music, new age music, each with its own style, seem to have a different effect on people. The smell of fresh flowers in the spring and the taste of perfectly ripened strawberries also bring forth feelings of rightness and connectedness. Our senses tell us the state of our environment; our body knows what is good for it. If the environment is just right energetically, it fills us with feelings of love, warmth, beauty, and connectedness. When we pay attention to our senses, we begin to choose things that give us pleasure instead of pain.

Although many people have never thought about themselves as a collection of energy, let's think about the skin, the largest sensing organ on our body. Somehow, even though we can use our eyes and see the physicality of our body, it is really composed of particles of energy. Matter or skin seems to be energy that is "slowed down" or made dense. It takes a lot of energy to make even a little bit of matter; it does seem it would take a lot of light beams to make up even one grain of sand. And a lot of molecules and sub-atomic particles to make up the entire surface of the skin on the human body. These particles combine together into atoms. Just the atom itself is an astounding concept. It has far more totally empty space in it than it has solid parts; about 99.99% empty space and that's what we are made of too. Could it be that the "energy" or consciousness flowing in this empty space is what makes the whole physical system work?

We are, on one level, a physical energy system playing in a physical domain. The physical body even has a consciousness that knows how to heal itself and how to balance its own chemical reactions. It even senses how we will grow and change as we move from birth to death. No matter how you look at your life, whether through the eyes of science or through the reality of your personal experience, you are surrounded by physical energies. When we integrate spiritual light into the physical body, it runs better, heals instantly, jumps higher, and it increases our ability to sense even more.

Instead of thinking of ourselves as a man or woman, white, black, yellow, or red, tall, thin, muscular, or frail, we can think of ourselves as a collection of energy. In fact a human being is so complex that we are actually a collection of energy systems. The physical body and the physical energies being one of those systems. Learning about ourselves as energy opens up a whole new arena of possibilities for human beings. We might even learn how magnificent we are and learn how to be comfortable with our physical bodies.

Emotional Energies

Emotions are a flow of "feelings" that inform our consciousness of what energy we are experiencing. When we see things that are beautiful we feel uplifted or see things that are horrific, we experience feelings of fear and despair. Emotions range from being bright and happy to dark and dismal depending on what we experience and how we perceive that experience. Emotions are meant to be sensed and evaluated and then allowed to flow again through our energy system.

At times we experience the energy of anger or the energy of love and these feelings tell us how we are perceiving the world. No matter how good or bad we feel emotionally over time, we would not really know how to negotiate in our life without our feelings. Knowing, on an energy level what to be joyful about and what to be afraid of is part of how we survived as a species. Emotions are a total impression of a situation that comes from summing up of all our sensory and internal states. When you experience the sun shining and it's your day off and your partner loves you, it feels good.

Emotional flow is even more than that. Feeling the energy in yourself and in others is part of the life force energy. If we cut ourselves off from feeling our emotions, we begin to die, because we have cut ourselves off from a big part of our own energy. The more we allow ourselves to feel our emotions the more alive we actually become.

We human beings are in the habit of holding on to our old negative emotions, blocking the natural flow of this energy. We do not like feeling negative emotions. Too many people close themselves off emotionally so they do not feel pain, depression, fear, etc. Despite the seeming advantage of not feeling intense pain, closing ourselves off emotionally has a terrible side effect. You also cannot feel joy, love, gratitude, acceptance, and peace with any intensity either. And you become a kind of zombie, able to interact with the world, but at a level so much less than you could otherwise. We all know some people like this. We say, "They don't have a clue". They are disconnected from their emotional energy body.

Can it possibly be good to feel things like sadness, grief, anger, and the like? Yes. Yes. A thousand times yes! Understand that there is a distinction between **feeling** an emotion and **acting out** an emotion. The feeling is our internal state that no one else may know about or understand. It is personal. How we act based on this internal state goes beyond the realm of the solely personal. Behaviors often involve other people. When acting, we must balance respect and love for ourselves with respect for other people, animals, plants, and objects involved.

Sometimes you may get confused when you feel an emotion. You may feel like you must act on it or you will explode. You always have the power of choice and can choose not to act on an emotion, instead observing and learning from this energy. We believe it is good to feel angry at your parents, even very angry, even furious. It is your life force expressing to you the energy of what you have just experienced internally. This has value for you. It doesn't matter what anybody else thinks, the feeling is really a gift to yourself. Just like the physical body will tell you when it is tired, your emotions will tell you when you are angry. But. But. A thousand times but. Throwing a negative emotion on someone else usually causes pain for you and for them. We suggest learning new ways.

In our culture, we want to hide from our feelings. We even want to hide from being too joyful. As beings of energy coming into full awareness, **we cannot grow and hide from our feelings at the same time.** We all need to learn how to observe and flow with our various emotional states. This part of our system is always changing and is very dynamic. To become a Young Old Master or an Old Young Master we must experience, learn from, and expand the flow of our emotional energy system. When you begin to view emotions as energy, from a detached point of view, your ability to cope with and appreciate powerful feelings can be greatly enhanced. Like different colors are different vibrations of light, different emotions are different vibrations of energy in your system.

Negative emotions have a lower vibration. Let's face it, there is a big difference vibrationally between depression and ecstasy. Feeling love and joy in our life is what makes us want to live. These feelings give us energy. Hatred, fear, and sorrow tend to drain our physical energy. We can choose to be in more positive emotions by becoming more conscious. Meditation is one of the tools that can be used to expand consciousness and awareness. Meditation can teach us how to release negative emotions on the energy level and blend with the higher vibrations, especially the vibration of love.

Love is the most powerful emotion we have. True love, spiritual love, transcends all other states of being. Love holds the highest energy vibration. If we consciously move love through our emotional energy system, it adds flow and expands the harmony we can feel. Our higher self wants us to live in a loving emotional state. This does not mean we ignore the other (lower) vibrations, rather it means we become more conscious and choose the vibration of love more often. In the core of our being is the beautiful steady vibration of pure love energy waiting to be released throughout all our systems.

As you learn more about yourself emotionally, you will have more personal freedom in life. Your emotional energy system will flow and your personal life will flow.

Mental Energies

To have a great life, most successful people have to become aware of their thoughts. In our group, we talked about the fact that what we put out on the mental level is what we receive back from the Universe. For example, if you "think" you are screwed up, your life will reflect that. However, if you "think" you are a beautiful being of love and light, your physical life will reflect that energy. Many teens have low self esteem, they don't think highly of themselves. But you know what? That doesn't really matter, because we have the ability to create new thoughts. Some old thoughts are stubborn, and we may have to work on releasing them, but with persistence, even stubborn negative thoughts can be changed.

Why don't you try this: Sit quietly and allow your mind to bring up a negative thought about yourself. For example, you may think I'm no good, I'm ugly, or I'm fat, no one likes me. Close your eyes and get in touch with that negative thought you have about yourself. After you are aware of this thought, feel the energy of this thought. Is it low, depressing, negative, dark? Sense where you feel the energy of this thought in your physical body. Is it in your stomach, heart area, throat, or head?

Our consciousness, the thinking part of ourselves, is an energy field that affects our thinking, our emotions, and our body. If we have a lot of negative thoughts about ourselves and our life, we live in a lower energy or a darker energy field. Of course, positive thoughts carry more light and have a higher vibration. The point is that we do have the choice to change our thoughts and live in more light. Even if we have terrible parents and bad karma and ugly hair, we can still choose to change the way we think about these things.

One of the greatest gifts our mental energy has to give us is the power to create. This power lies in the fact that we can change our thinking. All new ideas for TV shows, computer technology, and advanced automobile design begin with a thought. Sometimes these thoughts flow naturally as one idea leads to another, for example, one computer program builds on the next, and so on. Sometimes thoughts come in breakthrough ideas and something totally original is created. But we want you to remember, it is you, your parents, your neighbors, your cousins, the ordinary people, that have this ability to create. And everyone has the potential to have important breakthrough ideas. Thoughts are energy and we all have this creative energy field as a part of us.

One of the reasons we recommend meditation is that in the process of quieting our minds when we meditate, we create the potential for new ideas to come in. Also, as we relax our mental energy, we can more easily let go of negative thoughts. Our minds are always shifting and changing and are very active creating many thoughts, some negative, some positive. As we learn how to connect with our spiritual energy, our flow of thoughts can come from the higher wisdom and be more positive. Positive thoughts create a higher vibration. This draws in more positive energy to our life.

Sending our energy out through our thoughts and the act of focusing our mental energy does create results. But what we put out on the energy level is what comes back to us. As we work with energy to create, it is important to note that we recommend putting out only positive loving energy toward others as this is precisely what you will receive back in life. Your creative life energy is like a boomerang, so throw out exactly what you want to get back. Our history, books, and movies are full of the bad guy losing in the end or evil forces being destroyed by the good people. No matter how our life may seem at times, when some corrupt business people or drug dealers succeed, the real truth, the universal law is that man keeps evolving toward the higher, more positive vibrations. Humans continue to create loving thoughts because this energy feels better.

In the movie *Star Wars* it was clear to everyone that Darth Vader could not win in the end. The "Force" was with Luke Skywalker and this positive energy had to prevail.

Spiritual Energies

Sometimes the spiritual energy may be thought of as that "other" energy. It is the energy that goes beyond words, beyond logic, and beyond our regular emotions into a higher field of existence some people call the soul plane. When we learn to pay attention and sense the subtle cues we are given, we can know our spirit self or our soul. Our soul's energy is in every part of us. It can create physical healing and balance. It can help us communicate with god's wisdom through our thoughts. It is the energy we experience when we feel joy and love. We are always connected to our spiritual energy but we don't always realize the presence of our soul.

Every soul who comes to earth has a purpose. Part of everyone's purpose is to learn and grow. Our spiritual energy helps us learn and grow. Let's say we are attracted to partners who are not good for us. Your soul wants you to know you deserve to have a good relationship. So one way that humans learn is through pain because pain makes us uncomfortable and usually we want to shift out of pain in life. Your soul puts you in unsatisfying or painful relationships until you learn what kind of relationships are more satisfying or better for you. If you don't learn the first time, your soul or the universe that is connected to your soul keeps sending you painful relationships. Isn't your soul good to you?

Many things we experience in life are part of our purpose. Take a look at your life right now. You may be a student, work a part-time job, play sports, get good grades, have a great sense of humor, etc. It may not be obvious that this is what you are here to do right now. Quite often the things that bring us joy in life are part of our higher purpose such as creating a video for class, winning a basketball championship, or just going to a movie with friends. These can all be creative expressions of our spiritual energy. Our higher self is there to help guide us if we just pay attention.

We can learn through our spiritual energy how to live in joy rather than pain. The soul sends us gentle guidance and messages through the higher self. Remember our discussion about our gut feelings? If something doesn't feel right or is painful, your soul is trying to tell you something. You can learn to enhance your intuition (which is really subtle messages from your spirit self) by focusing your awareness on your spiritual self. It's fun and empowering to gain more insight, especially intuition into your own life. Many students have to make career or college choices. What if you could talk to your soul and see what the right decision is for you rather than learning by trial and error?

All people on the planet are getting more sensitive to the higher energies of their souls. This is a very good thing, because we can create a life with more joy and even create a world with more joy. Sometimes we get scared as we sense our spirit self, because it opens up more personal power. But this personal power can be used to enhance life, not destroy life. In our group the young masters enjoyed playing with their spiritual energy. Meg said, "It was kind of like discovering your sure or confident self. And you can feel more in tune with yourself and what your spirit wants for you."

Becoming a Master

It is amazing to think about all the energy of one human being. Do not judge your ability to become spiritual or spiritually integrated by what you think about yourself. All human beings have souls. All souls have tremendous unlimited potential. Even though you are young and fight with your parents, don't get along with your siblings, this does not diminish the fact that you have great potential. Part of your potential gets uncovered as you step on the path of self discovery. Learning about **all** of your energy is the secret to becoming a master.

To learn about yourself and connect more completely to the higher spiritual energies, it is important to get beyond your fear of God. Fear will stop you from accepting the greatness of your soul. Many religions focus on fearing God and God's punishments. When you make peace with God (or you might think of God as a being greater than yourself) as a loving source, there is much more spiritual light available for the body, emotions, mind, and spirit.

It is difficult for us as authors to convince you that giving up fear is a path to becoming more spiritual. You must have trust that this is true. As you grow and connect with the higher energies, you will come to know that this is a world of joy, and love and abundance, and a playground to explore your connection with every part of earth.

If you choose love and let go of fear, you will find God and be glad you did. Your body, emotions, and mind will align with the soul and your heart will sing.

The Playground

Time for some more fun out on the equipment. Be careful not to get hit in the head with a baseball!

Adventure and Explore

Remember to honestly say who you are with respect to the ideas or questions. There are no right or wrong answers; you don't even have to give one if you feel uncomfortable. Each person simply explores and expresses their own truth, either aloud or to themselves.

Let the game begin on the merry-go-round.

Round 1: Have you experienced any unusual coincidences since last time we asked?

Round 2: Have you ever felt a tingling outside of your body? Have you ever sensed anyone else's presence? Felt someone behind you and then turned around and found someone there?

Round 3: Have you ever felt an emotion while listening to music? Do different kinds of music make you feel different kinds of emotions? More people commit suicide who listen to country music than to other kinds. Can you guess why?

Round 4: Have you ever thought about someone and then they called you on the phone? Have you ever dreamt about someone and then they called you?

Round 5: Does my relationship with my boyfriend or girlfriend (my "body" friend) exist only on the physical level? Emotional level? Mental level? Spiritual level?

Round 6: Just within yourself, think about your boyfriend or girlfriend. How do you exchange energy on the four levels?

Round 7: What does it mean to have a physical connection with someone else? An emotional connection? An intellectual connection? A spiritual connection?

Create and Play

The rules in the game of life are complicated, but well worth learning.

Sensing the Strengths of Others

Some people have a strong emotional flow, some are gifted with expanded intellect, and some are connected to spiritual self. We all have our strengths and balances. When we are aware of energy, we can sense those strengths in others.

Have everyone in the group get quiet (or as quiet as you can) and pay attention to the energy in the room. Have each person write down, on a piece of paper, the name of the person in the group that is giving off the most intellectual energy. Don't go by reputation or your past impressions. Go by where you feel the energy in everyone at the moment. If you don't get a strong sensation, just relax a little and see who you would pick if you were just guessing. Remember to consider the possibility that it is you, yourself, that has this energy high.

Repeat this process for the most physical energy, the most emotional energy, and the most spiritual energy.

Compare notes and see how well you agree. Ask the person most often selected for a particular kind of energy to see if they thought they were giving off this kind of energy.

Sensing Negative Energy

Consider the five negative emotions of anger, fear, depression, resentment, and arrogance. Pair up with a partner and choose one of you to be designated A and the other B. Without speaking to each other, Partner A picks one emotion to radiate to Partner B. Partner B tries to sense which of the five emotions is being sent. Switch roles and try again.

Sensing Positive Energy

In a manner similar to the last game, consider the positive energy in the emotions labeled happy, peaceful, friendly, and loving. Pair up with a partner and choose one as A and the other as B. Partner A picks one of the positive energies to radiate to Partner B. Partner B tries to sense which energy is being sent. Switch roles and try again.

Does your ability to sense energy strengthen with practice?

Touch and Sense

In this section, we encourage you to play with meditation using affirmations. An affirmation is a single sentence of your choice that is used as a focus for the meditation. We suggest you focus your awareness on the integration of the body, mind, emotions, and spirit with a phrase like "I am one with my soul" or "My body, emotions, mind, and spirit work together in peace and harmony" or "I love all the parts of my being."

Meditation can be done in silence, but we have found that for people new to meditation, having music in the background makes it easier. Participating in a meditation is allowing yourself to explore your inner world. Some people are able to experience color, light, images, or physical sensations through meditation. But know that on any given day for any particular person, you may feel nothing, or your mind might be filled with the day's chatter. Don't worry about that, just let today's meditation be what it is. Tomorrow's will be different.

Guided meditations are meant to help you to relax, experience being with your own internal energies, and have fun. If you do not enjoy meditating or don't want to meditate, then don't. Just listening to tapes without trying to meditate will give you much benefit.

It is now time to listen to a guided meditation journey. Get yourself in a comfortable physical position, sitting or lying down in a quiet room. Be ready to play a tape in its entirety, which takes about 30 minutes. Try to find a time and space when you will not be interrupted. Turn off the phone and the pagers. Some people light a candle to help them prepare a quiet inner space.

CHAPTER 4  Sensing Energy

Part of growing spiritually is developing the ability to sense your own vibration. Sensing your own spiritual energy takes practice and focus and can be thought of as developing an extra-ordinary sense. It is easy to learn how to sense energy through nature's vibrations. When you practice feeling the strength and beauty of the mountains or the rolling power and vastness of the ocean, you can expand your ability to sense your own spiritual energy.

Our Fun and Games Together

We began our evening by talking about sensing the energy in our natural surroundings. We explained to the group that all people can learn to sense energy. In the novel, *The Celestine Prophecy*, the main character finds himself in a special place where research is being done on sensing the aura (energy) around plants. As he spends time in the special garden, he begins to "see" auras around plants and people. The researchers are studying the effect of meditating and projecting energy into plants to increase the light in their auric field. We asked our young people if anyone had ever seen or sensed energy around a favorite tree or plant? Each person in the group could identify with sensing "something different" when they were in or near some natural surroundings.

Everything is made up of energetic vibrations. Nature is constantly emitting subtle energy from plants, trees, rocks, rivers, canyons, mountains, and seas. We as humans respond to this natural energy; it is not unusual to feel drawn to the beauty of the mountains, the vastness of the oceans, and the peace of the deserts. It is as if nature is speaking to us through the positive feelings we get when we experience natural beauty. We are sensing the language of nature's vibrations.

In our group we began to practice sensing energy by experimenting with crystals and natural rock. We gathered together a collection of quartz crystals, amethyst, and Michigan rock from Lake Huron. All the group members were asked to close their eyes and imagine they were getting peaceful and centered; upon opening their eyes they chose the stone that most drew their attention. Sometimes the prettiest crystals were not the stones that drew them energetically, rather they were the ones that felt right.

We used this exercise to point out that different crystals have different vibrations, each stone emits a different energy. We also have our own unique vibration. Quite often we are attracted to a particular natural element because of the energy it is transmitting to us. This natural energy may have a similar vibration to ours or its energy enhances our own vibration. Our soul signals us to pay attention to the places or things in nature that gives us energy and increases our vibration.

These young adults were amazed that they could actually sense some subtle energy in the crystals they chose. They also knew intuitively which stone was right for them. After we had chosen our crystals and sensed their energy, we began a second exercise by passing the crystals around the room to the person on the left. With each new stone in hand, we would stop, focus our attention, and sense its vibration.

Sensing these vibrations was usually experienced by subtle feelings or lack of feelings within. It was surprising to find that each stone was different from the next and our ability to feel energy was getting stronger the more we did this exercise. We pointed out to the group that each person experiences these vibrations differently. Some people are visual and sense colors or mental pictures as they "tune in." Others feel energy in their physical body.

We then tried another exercise where we transmitted energy into the crystal we were holding by just using our imagination and sending it light. We again began passing the stones to the left. Each time we passed a crystal, we stopped and sent it light. Everyone agreed that the energy vibration in each stone began to increase and the energy in the room grew too. Not only did the crystal send out a vibration, but the stone seemed to absorb energy when we focused our own light into it. It appeared that there is a give and take of energy in nature, and we are a part of this flow.

In the second half of our group session, we experimented with sensing and sending energy to each other. We began by explaining that there are spiritual energy centers in the body called chakras and that these centers are part of our sensing system. It is possible to experience the chakras through meditation, focus, and study. What we wanted to experiment with was sending and receiving energy to and from each other through our chakras; sensing spiritual energy inside and outside of the physical body. Since no one in the group really knew anything about the chakras, we were not sure that they would actually feel energy in their centers, but it seemed like an interesting experiment.

We had the young people partner with each other, choosing an A and B for this exercise. To make it simple, we asked them to picture an energy center in their partner located in the abdomen, the heart, the throat, or the third eye in the center of the forehead (see the diagram on the next page drawn by Meg). The group members were asked to close their eyes and sit face to face but not touching. They were then asked to focus on the energy centers of their partner.

We asked them to sense intuitively which center could use more light. We had partner A transmit to partner B by sending energy to the chosen energy center. They could do this by using their imagination. Without speaking, partner B could sense where partner A was focusing energy and light, and they were correct most of the time. As they switched partners and practiced this exercise, each person noticed they became more aware and sensitive to the energy being transmitted.

There was a feeling of surprise and amazement in the group as we went through this exercise. They knew they were sensing spiritual energy. They were using their intuition and it was working! To feel energy flow in your body by having someone send you light gave everyone a new sense of power. If you try this exercise, you may notice that you feel lighter when you receive energy and often feel more expanded when you send energy. One member of the group commented that he could feel energy everywhere.

We want you to know that you have great abilities to work with energy and spiritual light to enhance your life and the lives of many others. It begins by increasing your awareness, concentrating, and practicing. Sensing energy is a matter of paying attention to your own subtle internal feelings. All people need to learn to value feelings because, just like coincidences, they are helping you know your world.

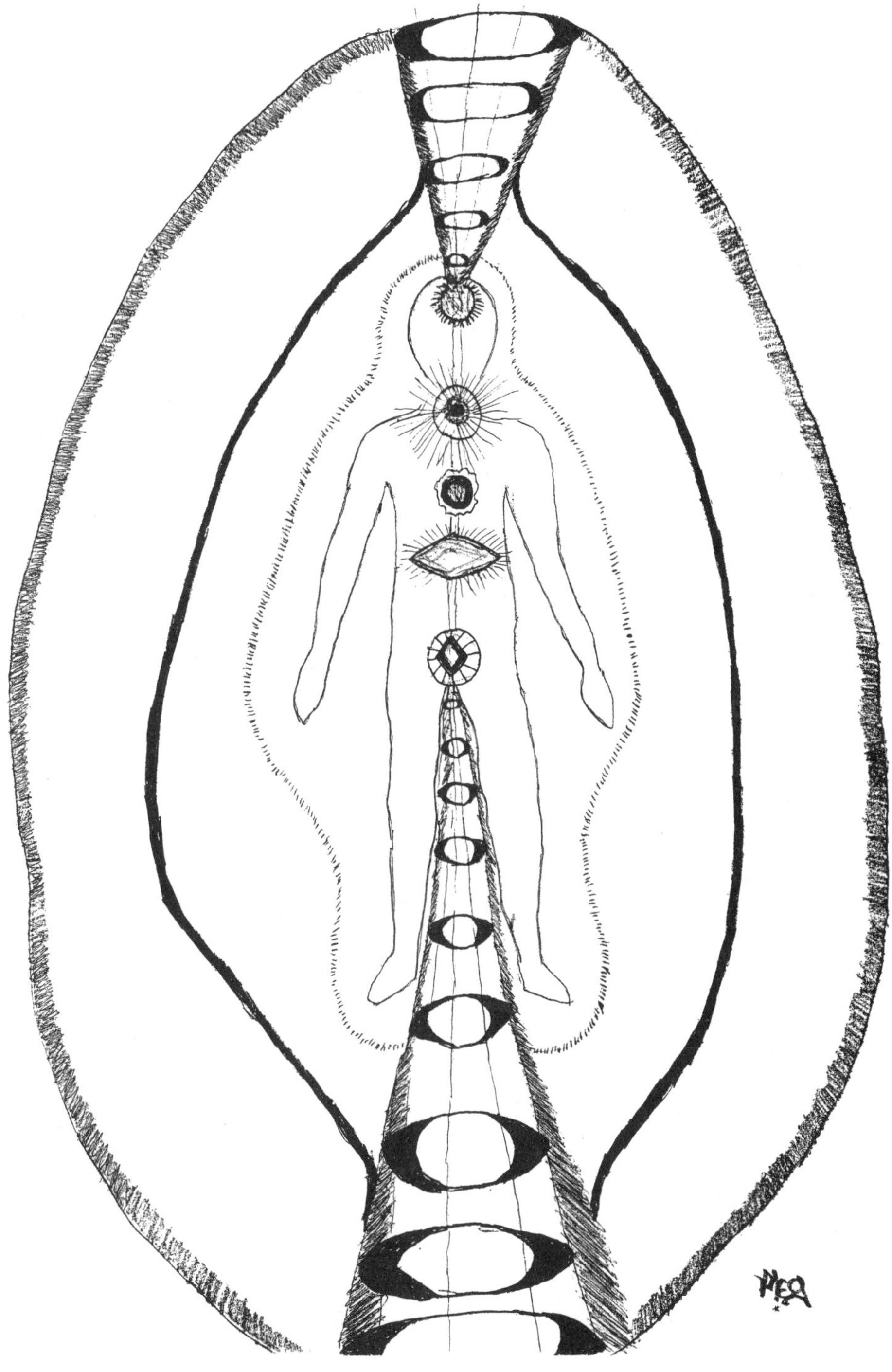

Being able to sense the energy in nature, your own energy, and then the energy of others will expand your ability to fully connect the body, mind, emotions, and spirit.

When you become more aware energetically, you will realize that the planet itself is sending you energy. As you grow spiritually, you will strengthen your connection to your higher self and this is a way to have all the energy you need in life. By sensing the energy of the world and the spiritual energy of themselves, our young people began to discover they are more than just 17-year-old, hormonally charged bodies; they are souls. There is much to learn about life when you begin to explore energy.

Listen and Imagine

Earth Energy

All natural things have a vibration that calls to us in certain ways. For example, the sun has a very powerful energy that can shift our mood and warm our physical being when we connect to it. Children seem to know intuitively how to interact with nature. On a sunny day they may choose to play outside, swim in lakes or oceans, climb rocks and trees, or dig in the sand. They are connecting in a very real way with the earth energy. As adults we do some of the same things but get separated from nature in our day-to-day work life. We forget that connecting with the earth energy can restore a healthy balance in our physical bodies. Most people do know intuitively that connecting with nature is energetically empowering, no matter what age you are.

Have you ever just allowed yourself to feel the sand between your toes, focusing in a way that gives you a sense of the earth below? How does it feel when you are suddenly aware of your environment? There are special moments when the sun, sand, water, and sky come together in such a way that the beauty and peace of this connection feeds your soul. You can become energized experiencing nature, and Mother Earth is constantly sending us energy. This energy can help raise our vibration, but we don't always connect to it. When you increase your spiritual awareness, you may find that you become very aware of earth energy. It may become important for you to spend more time "soaking up" the energy and beauty of nature. These connections create inner peace and harmony and help you have a healthy body, mind, and spirit.

There are some other interesting qualities about connecting to the earth that we want you to be aware of. Have you ever been on a vacation and felt like you really belonged in the place you were visiting? Most of us have friends or relatives who live throughout the country or world. Many people state they "feel" better in one area or another. Mary shared with the group the fact that her sister moved from Michigan to Seattle, Washington 20 years ago. Being a person who loves to sail, loves to backpack and wants to live near the mountains, this part of the country spoke to her inner vibration. She felt in harmony with the energy of Washington state and moved there. Your natural environment adds energy to your life. In fact, many people feel they belong, energetically, in certain natural environments.

You will usually be more aware of your connection to family and friends, but if you pay attention to your own subtle feelings you will notice your earth connection too.

Have you ever felt an inner pull or an inner calling to live in a certain place? Have you ever wondered why this is true? Can you imagine being aligned to an earth vibration that exists in a different country or continent? You may already be living in the right place on earth for you.

We all have a particular internal vibration that defines and expresses who we are on the energy level. Each one of us is unique. There are places you will live that are good for your energy system. When we feel an inner call to live in a certain area, quite often it is because our vibration aligns with the earth energy transmitted in that area. This inner call can also be a signal transmitted by your soul because of the people you will meet and the lessons you will be going through in life. Your soul may want you to live in Washington rather than Michigan because it is part of your life's path. If this is true, you will feel as if you belong in that place on the planet.

You may have the opportunity to visit some of nature's "high energy" spots, and when this happens people often feel they have been "changed" by this experience. This change can be thought of as the raising of your vibration or being energized by earth's energy. In fact some of earth's power spots also become spiritual centers and are preserved so many can experience earth's beauty and peace. In the US and Canada some of the most beautiful and awesome parts of our continent are preserved as National Parks. Some of the same park areas were considered sacred ground by the Native American Indians. When you visit the Grand Canyon, the Canadian Rockies, Muir Woods, the Blue Ridge Mountains, or the Everglades, it is easy to feel the powerful energy of Mother Earth. Many people feel that they are more connected to God's energy when they experience these natural wonders.

The Native American Indians lived their lives feeling a deep spiritual connection to the earth. They sensed the subtle energies and strengths of animals, plants, sky, and earth. They did not separate themselves from the feel of the wind and rain, the spiritual aspects of the animal kingdom, and the healing power of certain plants and herbs. Rather, they joined with and were enriched by this energy; it became a part of their spirituality.

We can learn about our own energy through nature. Rivers teach us flow, mountains reflect strength, trees demonstrate being rooted, the sky exhibits openness, and wheat fields promote expansiveness. Look at your world. What are the earth vibrations saying to your soul? Do you feel connected to a special place? Like human beings, the earth is a collection of complex vibrations radiating and transmitting energy for our connection and evolution together. We are here on earth to learn, Mother Earth has much to teach us.

Becoming More Conscious About Energy

Our ability to sense energy has been and still is a vital part of our ability to survive. We know through vibrations interpreted by our feelings what things bring joy and peace. We also know how to sense denser vibrations, things that are dangerous, or things we fear. We even know how to sense what others are feeling, but sometimes we are not very aware. When people think they are not intuitive, this is just not true. They have buried their ability to sense energy below the conscious level but can **learn** how to become more sensitive and more aware. Becoming more conscious to the subtle energies of life is a way to become more intuitive and a way to learn how to read the energy of nature, animals, and other human beings.

The single greatest illusion that we all share is that we are separate: separate from each other, separate from the rest of our life, and separate from our soul's light. Living here on earth, it seems like we are each encased in our own body and that our bodies have very defined boundaries. When we are not aware of the subtle energies and when we are not aware of our soul's energy, we truly consider ourselves separate.

But let's consider this separation a little closer. It cannot be real from a physics point of view because we are all interconnected through the vibrations we send out and share. No one would argue about whether of not we feel the energy from the sun: just stand outside on a hot day. The transfer of the heat vibration is obvious. However, it is not as clear that when a person walks into a room, we all have an ability to sense the energy of this person. Yet we **know** that people emit energy and we **can** sense it. Our energies are considerably more subtle than the sun's but can definitely be felt and interpreted by learning skills of higher awareness.

Consider the following; have you ever eaten a peach at the peak of ripeness; soft and tender yet firm, filled with juice that runs down your chin the moment you bite into it? Have you ever sat near the ocean and listened to the waves, felt the wind on your face, heard the seagulls bantering in the sky, and watched the red skies of sunset fade into the evening? Have you ever walked deep into a pine forest on a summer day, felt the quiet, and experienced the clean scent descend upon you?

Why in the world do these things feel so good?

The answer is very simple. We are not alone. We are not separate. We are, in fact, part of all life, part of all existence.

Through energy vibrations and the principle of resonance we can know what is attracting us and what is repelling us. As we resonate with the vibration of the ocean, we become part of that experience through our spiritual energy. All of the pieces of life and existence intermingle in a complex play of energy where each aspect has its part. Even the energy of a beautiful, ripe peach has a vibration to share with our visual and physical body. When you are not aware of these interrelationships, you are missing some of the sacredness of life. You may be missing some of the joy and love you can experience here on earth when you are not aware of the energetic connections you have to people, nature, and things.

The people we meet, the places we choose to live, and the culture we are born into become a part of our personal resonance: the vibration of who we are. We share our energy with our family, friends, the animals, and plants in our environment. When we resonate with a certain natural environment, that part of nature has energy and consciousness to share with us. Our five senses help us sense subtle energy vibrations, but our spirit helps us know the meaning of this energy in our life. It is up to you to open your awareness and receive all that energy, wisdom, and meaning.

The personal physics of your life includes the fact that your soul is a source of limitless energy. It is an ever-present, everlasting, ever- vibrating source of unlimited energy. As it brings energy into us, our vibrations head out into the universe in waves of subtle energy. When our energy encounters energies from other sources, these energies interact. Sometimes the energies resonate together and the power of each is amplified by the other. At other times the energies clash, especially when they are vibrating at different levels and rates. You are drawn to the vibrations that resonate with yours and are repelled by the others.

As we have been discussing sensing the energy of the world and sensing the energy of who you are, we have two important concepts that are the focus of this book. 1) Everything is made up of energy vibrating at different frequencies, some higher, some lower; 2) To learn more about **yourself** as a being of energy, it is important to learn about the soul's energy and how it interacts with your physical body, your emotional energy, and your mental energy or the mind.

There are ways of learning more about yourself as energy and spirit. We have outlined two of the ways to learn about yourself in the next two sections. You can learn to become more intuitive and sensitive to the subtle energies of the soul. You can also learn how to transmit spiritual light to improve your life and the energy of the planet. As you read further about the spiritual energy centers of the body (the Chakras and the Light Body Centers), know that most people learn about these through a teacher and some form of meditation. Consider learning more about the Chakras or the Light Body because studying these forms opens doorways to your spiritual self and the spiritual aspects of earth's energy.

We are not saying you must learn these other systems of understanding spirituality, for there are many paths to the same end of "becoming enlightened." Because you are a master, honor and respect your choices in life. The path you choose is the one that is right for you, it is usually a path that raises your vibration.

We Are a World of Energy Within

Despite our lack of evidence, an intuitive healer named Caroline Myss suggests a perspective that fits precisely with that of this book: We are energetic beings. We are conduits for energy in and out of our body. In many different ways we take energy into ourselves, distribute that energy throughout our body, emotions, and mind and let the energy exit when we are complete. Ah, but the varieties and types and purposes of this energy are many. Therein lies the fascination and fun of life. We are a science of energy. Just as there is an order in the physical body that helps it run well, there is also an order to our spirituality, a science of spirituality.

Most people accept the simple fact that we are the most complex organisms on our planet. Every place else we look, other life is simpler. Compare a person to a rock, a person to a tree, a person to a dog, or a person to a chimpanzee. No matter where we look, we see simpler beings. As complex as human beings are, we can be studied and understood not only biologically but from a spiritual and energy perspective too.

Life's energy is a main factor in this complexity. We have no precise definition of life that we can prove is correct. Many would suggest that life is the connection of our soul to our physical body, but as yet we cannot prove that scientifically one way or the other. But most people would agree that when we die, "life energy" is no longer present in the physical body.

We know that our brain and nervous system provide one variety of energy that courses through our bodies. Small electro-chemical impulses begin at many places in our body and are then used to send information to other places in our body via nerve impulses. Perhaps you want to have a drink of water. Somewhere in your mind, you have registered a lack of adequate hydration internally. Your brain takes this intention and starts sending out wave after wave of neural messages urging you to stand up from your chair, walk into your kitchen, extract a glass from the dishwasher, place it under the faucet, pour some water, raise the glass to your mouth, and drink it. That is a tremendous number of neural pulses that had to go through your system to coordinate this complex (yet really relatively simple) task.

In another situation, the doctor during your physical exam takes that small hammer and taps your knee to test your reflexes. The hit on your knee creates a very specific neural message that starts to head toward your brain. This one, though, is a reflex and is almost immediately returned as a motor pulse to kick your leg without any conscious control. Many other neural activities are just as unconscious or autonomic, like keeping your heart beating or continuing to breath. Indeed, the amount of energy that zips back and forth in our nervous systems is astounding. Just think about the activity required to type this page. We are incredibly complex!

Of course, this does not even mention the other systems that exist within our body. Obviously there is the circulatory system controlling blood flow to every part of our body. The respiratory system controls the intake of oxygen and the release of carbon dioxide. We have an endocrine system, a digestive system, a lymphatic system, a skeletal system, a musculature system, etc. Yet with all of this complexity, when we compare one person to another, we are pretty much the same.

At this time in history, the Human Genome Project continues trying to unravel the meaning of every part of the human DNA. The project is funded by governments around the world. They are studying the DNA of one, single person, one man. His identity is not publicly known but he is supposedly of middle European heritage. Scientists throughout the world are trying to uncover all the meaning in every piece of his DNA. Why just his? Because at the genetic level, we are all 99.9% the same. The differences between race, gender, size, shape, intelligence, or any other characteristic you care to mention occur in less than 0.1% of our DNA. So the way our different body systems work is, not surprisingly, relatively similar one to another.

If it is not our biology that makes us different from each other, it must be something deeper within. It must be the soul's energy that creates the differences from one human to another. It could be our spirit that determines when one person will live as an artist in Spain and another person will live as a bricklayer in New York. The life force energy that we will call the soul holds the meaning and purpose of our life. But how is our soul's energy anchored and channeled through the body, emotions, and mind?

The Chakras

One system that works well to describe an energetic view of the body/soul connection is the chakra system. The belief in these energy centers comes out of ancient Eastern Asian religions in a time when scientific knowledge of the human body was much more limited than it is now. The original chakra system describes the human body in terms of seven energy centers located in the body.

These seven centers corresponded to seven locations of life energy in the body. The first one is at the base of the spine and then moves up from there. Learning about the chakras and learning how to sense energy in your chakras can help you become more aware of your life from an energetic perspective. The seven centers have been given many names. The ones we choose to use are the following:

Root chakra (muladhara) is located at the base of the spine. It is focused on the energy of survival and issues related to our physical world.

Sacral chakra (svadisthana) is associated with human sexuality. It is the source for creative energies and issues of birth and relationships.

Solar plexus chakra (manipura) is located in the "gut." This center is focused on ego. When things are going awry, it is our gut that gets twisted up, where the tension sits. This center is about the ego, self esteem, and power.

Heart chakra (anahata) is focused on issues of unconditional love and being a source of love in life; of compassion for ourselves and our fellow beings.

Throat chakra (vishuddha) is focused on issues of will, issues of self expression, and speaking the truth.

Third eye chakra (ajna) is an energy source focused on issues of the mind, intuition, insight, and spiritual sight.

Crown chakra (sahasrara) is the center for connections to spirit and opening yourself to a higher spiritual flow.

Is it reasonable for us in this "scientific" era to disregard this ancient system for understanding the human energy system? Probably not. We share virtually the same internal wiring as all of the people who worked over the centuries to conceptualize and refine these understandings. In some sense, the chakra system was developed in as systematic a manner as any other human model like chemistry or physics. While the ancient peoples did not have the measurement devices that we now possess, they could still develop hypotheses as to how their world was organized and then validate and test them against the truths they did possess, that is, the knowledge of their subjective experience of being human.

We have given you a basic overview of this system but there is much more to learn if you are interested. We suggest that you let your own inner guidance, your own intuition, tell you if you should study the chakras. Studying the chakras and the energy transmitted from these areas of the body can help you understand your inner strengths and some of your weaker areas in life. As you work on opening up blocked energy in the chakras, you can experience better health and a more complete understanding of your life. (See chapter 9 for resources.)

The Light Body Centers

We have talked about the chakras and now we want to introduce you to another level of energy awareness called the Light Body. *"Your light body is an energy body that exists at a higher level, closer to your soul energies than your chakras. It is your aura as it exists in the higher dimensions of your soul"* (writes DaBen and Orin). The "Awakening Your Light

Body" course, which teaches these energy centers was developed and produced by Duane Packer and Sanaya Roman who are channels for DaBen and Orin. (See Chapter 9 for further resources and information about their material.)

To awaken your light body, you learn a system of energy centers that align with the chakras but vibrate at a different energy level. After we completed our initial group sessions, Chris, Mary, and the Young Old Masters studied this system together. Before we learned about the Light Body, we did not realize these energy centers existed. But, just because we didn't know these centers were available does not mean they do not exist. One of the first things you discover when you play with your soul's energy is to be open to learning new things. Each time we work with the Light Body and the Light Body Centers, we learn more about the higher energies, strengthening spiritual connections, and how to bring more light into the physical world. This system has taught us how to increase our ability to sense spiritual energy.

The Light Body energy centers align with the chakras in the physical body and have unusual names.

> **Nu'a, Dinia, Leow,** and **Ranthia** are the first four centers and help to open and regulate emotional flow in your system. Do you remember our discussion about your emotional energy? These centers, when open and flowing, help create peace and harmony in your emotional energy system.

> **Treao, Pieah,** and **Renawre** are the next three centers and open your mental energy flow. Working with these centers can help you change negative

thoughts, let go of the past, and open up creativity and inner sight.

Fullonia, SaHa, and **Vee** are the spiritual centers that open doorways to your soul and beyond. They also open your awareness to the Light Body cocoon, a sphere of light beyond your aura, that holds your soul's energy. Working with these centers helps you access the higher spiritual planes and higher frequencies of energy and light.

This course is designed to blend more of the soul's energy with our four energy bodies, physical, emotional, mental, and spiritual. The Light Body centers are learned though tones, vibrations, and guided meditations.

Meditation is a key to increasing your ability to sense higher energies. Working with the chakras or the Light Body centers assists you in reaching deep meditative states. Each time you meditate, you expand your consciousness, blend with your soul, and increase your vibration. When you increase your vibration, you can sense the spiritual energies. In *The Celestine Prophecy,* the main character learned how to increase his vibration and could then "see" light around plants, trees, and people. If you want to get very good at sensing energy, you will probably need to learn how to meditate.

Different Paths - Same Energy

There are many people all over the world being called to grow spiritually. People from all walks of life in all countries are looking for ways to awaken. There are many different techniques and philosophies to choose from. None of these is

right or wrong. The different teachings each have a slightly different vibration. Guess what? You will be called to the teaching or philosophy that is right for you. Trust your inner voice. Remember you are the Master and you will know what is right for you.

Whether you choose to study the Chakras or take the path of "Awakening Your Light Body", the path of Christianity, the path of Buddhism, the path of Judaism, or the path of Islam, all spiritual growth attempts to awaken man to his or her highest potential by aligning with a higher power. If you are not aligned vibrationally to the path you are on, it will not be very effective for your spiritual growth. This is why everyone must choose their own path and we as humans must learn to honor the choices of others. This is the best way to raise your own vibration, through your own highest path. We all need to respect each others' choices to raise the vibration of the planet.

No matter which religion or spiritual growth path you choose, when you align with your soul, you become a being of higher light, a transmitter of positive energy. This positive energy and spiritual light changes the vibration of your own life, your family, your friends, your neighborhood, your village, your state, your country, and the world. As many people, through their own sacred paths, increase their personal light around the planet, this group light becomes more available for healing, love, and a joining together as one.

The Playground

Time for some more fun out on the playground. Today we are going to go outside to play.

Adventure and Explore

As usual, we want to give you some questions for you or for a group discussion. Remember there are no right or wrong answers; you don't even have to give one if you feel uncomfortable. Each person simply explores and expresses their own truth, either aloud or to themselves.

Round 1: Picture your favorite natural setting, whether it be a mountain, a beach, a forest, or a starry sky. How do you feel inside when you connect to nature outside?

Round 2: If you and a friend both pictured the same setting, such as ocean waves on a beach, does it feel the same for both of you or different?

Round 3: When you sense any disharmony in your own body or emotions, what happens when you connect to nature?

Round 4: What place on earth or natural setting has the most healing energy for you?

Round 5: If you are feeling stressed out, in what part of your body do you feel the stress? If you are feeling happy, what part of your body holds the happiness for you?

Round 6: Have you ever felt energy flowing from your heart? From your other chakras or energy centers?

Create and Play

Remember to play with the energy. Know that your experiences are valid and you are not making this up when you sense higher energies.

Sensing the Energy of Nature

Gather together some crystals, natural rock, plants, flowers, feathers, leaves, sea shells, or whatever natural items are available.

If you are working in a group, place the items in the center of the circle. Have all members of the group close their eyes, get quiet, and focus on connecting with the energy of the natural items in the center.

Have each member take one item from the center, one that they seem to be attracted to energetically, something that draws their attention. Each member is then instructed to close their eyes, focus on their item, and see if they can sense a subtle vibration or feeling.

After a few minutes, each person should pass their item to the person on their left and try to sense the energy of a new natural item. These feelings are subtle, but they are real. Pay attention to how you experience each of the different items as they go around the room. Some people experience energy by getting pictures, colors, sounds, etc. in their mind. Some people experience energy by feelings. Some people experience physical sensations. Notice how you experience the energy.

As you pass the items, did you notice anything happening

to the energy in the room? Did your ability to sense these subtle energies increase as you practiced more? Did you have trouble sensing any energy? **Remember you are just learning. You may not feel or sense anything at first.**

Experiment with transmitting some of your energy into these natural items and then sensing what you experienced throughout this process. Practice transmitting energy and passing the items around your circle. Sometimes we played soft meditation music in the background and this helped the group get into a relaxed, receptive state of awareness.

Sensing Energy in Each Other

As we described in the first section of this chapter, people can even practice sensing the energy centers of each other.

Choosing a partner A and a partner B, have people in the group create pairs, sitting face to face. Begin this exercise by getting into a quiet, centered space. Play some meditation music, lower the lights in the room, and light a candle or two. Partner A will sense the energy of partner B. Partner B will open to receive energy into their chakras or energy centers.

First partner B will sit quietly and sense which center in their body needs more energy, the root, sacral, solar plexus, heart, throat, third eye, or crown chakra. Then Partner A will sense partner B, taking your time, notice which energy center draws your attention. Picture sending light to that center simply by using your imagination and creative visualization. Partner B will notice any feelings, sensations, or pictures they receive during this transmission. Each pair should take five minutes to focus on sending and receiving.

The pair will then discuss their experience. What did it feel like to sense the energy of your partner and send light? What did it feel like to receive energy from your partner?

Could you sense your own energy centers? Did your partner sense which energy center could use more light?

Next, switch roles and partner B will transmit to partner A and discuss your experiences when the exercise is complete.

How difficult or easy is it to sense energy?

Touch and Sense

It is time for another meditation. You've had the opportunity to try silent meditations, unfocussed meditations, meditations with affirmations, meditations with or without music, and maybe even guided meditations. From now on the choice is up to you - remake the decision every time you meditate.

You may want to try a nature journey today, experimenting with a tape that has sounds of nature, connecting with those vibrations and tones that connect with our natural environment.

Explore your inner world. Experience color, light, images, or physical sensations. Know that on any given day, you may feel nothing, or your mind might be filled with the day's chatter. Don't worry about that, just let today's meditation be what it is. Tomorrow's will be different.

The guided meditations are meant to help you to relax, to experience being with your own internal energies, and to have fun. Perhaps you want to listen to the tapes without trying to meditate. Play with the meditations, creating the best experience for you.

CHAPTER 5 🌿💜 Energy of Relationships

In all relationships there is a give and take of energy. In an evolved relationship, the energy flow is balanced and loving. One way in which we learn about ourselves is by interacting with other people. It is through our relationships that we learn how to love and how to be loved. Your life is full of different relationships and it becomes important as you grow spiritually to be clear and authentic in your relationships; to know and speak your truth; to feel sure and confident in your ability to share energy with others.

Our Fun and Games Together

In *The Celestine Prophecy,* the author explores the concept of stealing energy. People want energy and power. Not believing we have an inner source of power, we often "steal" energy from each other. Most of the time, we are not aware we are doing this. We steal through force, manipulation, being the good guy, being the bad guy, being poor me or the hero. You may be very familiar with power struggles, having battled others to gain control or keep control in your own life. But maybe you have never thought of these power struggles as seeking energy. In our group we tried an exercise that had the young people experience "the struggle for power."

We asked the group members to do a simple request/decline exercise. The members broke up into groups of two, one designated as A, the other designated as B. Partner A was to request something from partner B. Partner B was to politely decline, **just say no**. We asked partner A to make this a simple request like, "Will you wash my car?" or "Will you lend me a dollar?" Partner A was to keep asking partner B for the same thing for about 5 to 10 minutes. All throughout the exercise, partner B was to just say no. Partner A requests and partner B declines. Sounds simple, doesn't it?

What happened next was a classic struggle for power. As A requested and B declined, we saw all the energy stealing techniques they knew come into the exercise. There was in-depth explaining going on, there was manipulating, there was even begging and pleading. Some A's even threatened B's to cave in and say yes. It was really funny to observe the immediate conflicts as one person withheld energy from the other. Partner B's held their ground but felt the very strong pulls on their energy.

As they switched roles and the exercise proceeded, we asked each person to see if they could observe which scenario seemed most common for them. Were they the type to try and dominate the other? Or manipulate the other? Or just give in to the other? In any case, we all began to "feel" the struggle for power. The pulling of energy back and forth was comical to observe and it was clear if B would just say yes to A, the struggle would end.

Both groups admitted they had trouble holding their own center, holding their own energy intact. Why do we believe that we must steal energy to survive? Why do we believe we do not have our own supply of energy within? Why do we feel we must say yes to another person's request even if we don't want to?

Todd stated that he could see clearly how young guys go about stealing energy from each other by physically beating on each other to gain power or by "cutting down" the other guy. Meg saw that she steals energy by being aloof and holding back, making others come to her rather than easily sharing her energy. We have some funny beliefs about ourselves, such as, "I am weak," "I need energy," "I am powerless", or "the only way to be powerful is to dominate." These beliefs set up an unconscious pattern of stealing energy. We know we need energy to live and look outside of ourselves to get it.

In our group we discussed the fact that when you steal another person's energy, this is only a quick fix. Stealing energy will only solve the problem temporarily. Because we do not believe that the Universe has an unlimited supply of energy for us, we are constantly faced with stealing more. All of this is usually exhausting because we are looking for energy, for love, for security, or protection outside of ourselves. Whether you steal energy or readily give your energy away by being the victim, it is exhausting on both sides. The young people agreed it would be better if we knew there was a higher source of energy within and we drew our power from our inner source.

As a group we discussed our own relationships. Some people are intimidators forcing others to give them energy. Some people are victims, playing the "poor me", so others will give them energy. Most people know intuitively they would like to have a more evolved relationship where the energy is exchanged in a balanced manner. Quite often in the group we created more questions than answers not really knowing

how to create balanced relationships. We are all exploring, in our own way, how to have better relationships. Seeking love through stealing energy is not soul love, the kind of love that feeds energy to our soul and makes our heart open to more light.

We closed our group with a meditation focusing on letting go of other peoples' energy and letting our own higher self fill us with light. It was an interesting evening and Brian, Craig, Meg, Todd, and the others began looking at their own patterns of behavior in relationships. Someone mentioned that if we all knew we could get energy from our soul, we would not be so dependent on each other. There would be no need to struggle and fight for energy. As we were all contemplating what we had just experienced we went into a meditation and experienced our soul sending us energy and light. It was a powerful meditation and a powerful lesson.

We come onto this planet to have relationships, to be a part of a community with other people here, and to grow through a balanced interdependence. Having relationships is what life is all about. Friends, lovers, parents, work associates, and soul mates can all enrich our lives. Relationships are part of our spiritual growth. A major part of our learning here on earth is how to have a relationship and keep our own energy intact. How do we share love, time, and energy with others without power struggles and stealing energy? How do we trust and love our own inner source?

Everything is energy, even our relationships have energetic qualities. As you explore who you are as a being of energy, it is important to look at what is going on spiritually for you and the people in your life.

Listen and Imagine

Friend Relationships

One of the magical qualities about friends is that we get to pick our friends consciously. We like them, and we don't have the same conflicts of energy with them that we have with our parents, brothers and sisters. It can be said that friends have a like vibration. We are attracted to each other because of a core energy we share. We have a connection to our friends, an energetic connection. Friends love us for who we are, not in spite of who we are. Friends are part of our spiritual community here on earth.

In the television show "Seinfeld", when you observe how Jerry, George, Elaine, and Kramer interact, you begin to see that they accept things in each other that they would never accept in their families or romantic partners. This is certainly a big part of the power of friendship in life. Friends accept us, warts and all. A best friend usually shares their energy freely with us and there are similar vibrations we share in common. When your best friend likes a certain new CD, you usually like it too. You share the same beat in life, walk to the same drummer. Friends are also our teachers. There is something important we will learn about ourselves from each friendship we have.

You will learn self love from your friends. You will learn how talented you are from the friends who see more in you than you can see in yourself. Friends encourage your growth and life dreams and they laugh at your jokes. Many times a friend understands the meaning of your life better than you do.

There is a joy and a "laughing at life" that you can have with your friends. At some of life's worst moments, you have called your friends and laughed about your terrible problems together. At times a friend may be the only one who will understand how a great event affects you. As you learn to look a little deeper at relationships, you will become aware that your soul knows the soul of your friend. Imagine your soul talking to the soul of a friend and setting up the energy exchange that will flow between you. Friends are a part of your higher guidance in life, bringing you messages at the right time and in an acceptable manner.

We are not trying to say that all friendships and relationships are perfect. Power struggles and stealing energy goes on between friends. You will have power struggles with your friends and they will mirror bad habits back to you. Sometimes your buddy will say something really annoying and you will realize you said the same thing yesterday. Friends teach us about ourselves.

You are an energy vibration and so are other people. Some of the reason people are attracted to each other is because of the energy they share. Our Young/Old Masters discovered that they have an energetic connection. As you explore energy, you will discover your spiritual connection to others and uncover the true meaning of your relationships. Even when you are not aware, your spiritual energy is leading you to the people, places, and things that will help you grow. Friendships assist in raising our vibration, encouraging our growth, and teaching us about ourselves.

As we all seek to add more love to our lives, friends freely share that vibration with us. As we connect with one special person who becomes our partner in love, our own learning about the energy and power of love grows to a new level.

Lover Relationships

In some love relationships, we have strong physical attractions but no deeper personal love. In others we may have deep loving vibrations, like a soul connection, but no strong physical sexual drive. Some relationships contain elements of both. In all relationships, we bond together to learn about ourselves but we don't always realize this at the time. We plug our energy into our partners and they plug their energy into us and we call this love. It is fun, exciting, and confusing all at the same time. As you evolve spiritually, the type of close personal relationship you want in your life may change and grow.

In fact you and your partner may grow together into a relationship that is connected on the physical, emotional, mental, and spiritual levels.

Some of our first love relationships are primarily physical attractions. We get excited on the physical level when we see or are near this person. Our sexual energies get aroused and sometimes we call this physical, sexual connection being in love. However this can also be described as "being in lust." As you get to know your partners emotions and mind, you may realize the physical connection is not enough to sustain a long-term relationship. We are complex beings who are seeking deep loving connections and usually a strictly physical relationship will not satisfy our soul.

People also become connected because of the emotional needs they meet in each other. A person who feels good when they rescue someone else will often partner up with a victim who needs rescuing. We join in these relationships to learn about our own emotional needs and how to meet them spiritually instead of creating dependency on each other. A dependent type relationship is filling an emotional void within. We seek to fill an empty feeling, using emotional energy experienced through our partner. These emotionally dependent relationships do not always last unless both partners can learn from each other and evolve to a higher way of relating. Meeting each others' emotional needs is not a bad thing. But being overly dependent blocks the natural spiritual flow of energy that can happen for two people in love. People can share love with each other but cannot meet **all** of each others needs.

As you get to know your lover, it is usually important to have some common beliefs and thoughts you both share. This is part of what keeps people connected even when things "get tough" in the relationship. People from the same cultures, religions, and types of families know naturally how to relate to each other. The way you think and the way your partner thinks can be important to getting along with each other. We create realities with our mental energy. When two people join together in a love relationship, and have opposite thought processes, their mental energy is at war. Understanding and accepting your partner's thoughts and beliefs helps the relationship grow even if you do not completely agree. People who think differently can complement each other. However, having some shared basic values, such as the same cultural or religious beliefs, helps make day-to-day living together easier.

The Power of Love

Earlier in the book we talked about people seeking "loving energy." The one-on-one love relationship we set up with our girlfriend or boyfriend is very important to young adults. In fact, the lover relationship probably remains the most important relationship for people of all ages. We experience the vibration of loving spiritual energy through our love relationships. The intense feelings of joy, passion, and "being in love" are spiritual energies. These feelings are soul vibrations. For some people having a loving relationship with another **is** the meaning of their life and helps them experience spiritual love.

When a relationship is this profound and exciting, it isn't surprising how much we talk about it, joke about it, study it, get offended by it, and yet still enjoy it. One thing is for sure, when you are involved in a love relationship, you know that you are alive. People feel joy, deep connections, and physical sexual attraction. They feel their heart open and the energy of love flow through the body, emotions, and mind. Experiencing love is a spiritual experience. If you start to view your relationships from an energetic perspective, you can understand how to create more openness and a greater spiritual flow of love between you and your partner.

Imagine a young couple. They look into each other's eyes and see only love. At every opportunity, they hold hands, they touch, they kiss. As the day progresses, each one feels the desire to tell the other about the details of the day, what has been good, what has been bad, how they are doing. When they meet, they are able to become present to each other, putting aside the confusions of the day and focusing in that very moment. The awakening of a loving vibration within themselves is sparked by the loving vibration within their partner.

Energetically, lovers share their energies. Each is willing to spend a portion of their life energy on the other. When you take the time to be with someone, say you go out to a movie on a Saturday night, you are choosing to spend some of your energy with and on that person. As both partners in a lover relationship spend their energies on each other, each experiences the energy of love, the life force energy that helps us know our true higher self. When we have an evolved relationship, the energy of love flows freely and each person makes choices that are in their own highest good. In this kind of shared love, people can grow into their own highest potential.

Consider the simple phrase "filled with love." On the best day of any romantic relationship, we all can momentarily reach this place. A place of completion. A place of contentment and peace. A place where we feel no need for any future time, no worry about any past time, and are content to be just who we are, where we are, experiencing that moment of our lives. If each person in a love relationship can draw loving energy from within, the relationship can be created from choice instead of need. This relationship can then be "filled with love" from the self instead of from the other. The relationship can evolve to a higher level and be filled with spiritual light.

A relationship that is pure joy is a relationship that exists in the energy of freedom. Freedom to be exactly who you are and feel loved for who you are. To live, play, and love in the energy of freedom, each partner must evolve beyond their dependencies and know that they are the source. You are the source of your power. You are the source of loving energy in your life. You are a student learning skills that lead to enlightenment. Your partners, your lovers, and your friends are your teachers and helpers in life but not your source. When you fully know you are the source for our own life, then you can have sacred loving relationships. You will choose a partner who enhances your energy. You will choose a partner who is already filled with love.

Love heals. Feeling loved can transform our lives. Love has the power to conquer many obstacles and create an opening so we can know God's love for us. As we blend with a partner and experience love, we are experiencing our own soul's energy. When we are "in love," it is a physical, emotional, and spiritual experience. This is why relationships are so powerful. We are living in the essence energy of our soul when we are in the energy of love.

Soul Relationships

It can be said that all relationships are soul relationships. All the people in your life bring you messages, coincidences, and learning experiences. In our close relationships, we somehow know (sense) each other and we realize there is a connection. But there are some relationships that go beyond time and space. They are more special, and the connection to each other pulls us onto our higher path. Why is that true? As you grow spiritually and are able to sense the higher energies, you will see that some relationships are the most empowering for you in life. It seems like their soul talks to your soul. The words, the activities, and the love you share shapes your life and you know your life would not be the same without their presence.

In *The Celestine Prophecy*, the main character kept meeting the just-right people who would lead him to the next insight. If we allow our soul to guide us, the same thing will start happening. If you say to your soul, "I am ready to be on my highest path," some very interesting soul relationships will appear along with teachers and guides. Some people call these teachers, friends, and lovers their "soul group." We believe you have a group of people here on earth that you are energetically connected to and a group of higher beings that you are also connected to. Both groups are here for your growth and higher awareness. It is up to you to pay attention.

As you commit to your spiritual journey, some relationships will leave your life as you no longer need that person for your growth. But other relationships, where you have a powerful soul connection, will come into your life and benefit you and the other person as well. A soul relationship feels strong, it feels loving, it often feels challenging, and it has a higher vibration. It matches the vibrations that you are evolving to. Sometimes there is synchronicity in your thoughts, feelings, and perceptions of the world. Often your soul friends assist you very directly in your spiritual growth. They know what you need even before you know.

In a more evolved soul relationship, there is what we would call a "higher love," a blending of the higher wisdom with the healing vibration of love. Soul relationships create the vibration of a loving flow that empowers each person to go even higher. We can have soul-to-soul relationships with our lovers and become more conscious of the energy we are giving and taking. This type of love endures, even if people do not stay committed to each other. In soul relationships, each person must follow their own highest path and continue to evolve. We are now in a time of exploring what it means to have more evolved relationships.

Look at your present relationships. Which of those touch you deeply? When you meditate, can you connect with the soul of another? We are asking questions for you to explore the meaning of your life as a body, mind, and spirit and the meaning of your connection to others. When you begin to look at your relationships as two souls coming together for mutual learning, how you perceive much of your life changes. The struggle for power changes into the challenge to grow beyond the struggles in life. If you want power and you want flowing relationships, reach upward. Ask your higher self, "What am I here to learn?" When we drop the struggle for dominance, control, manipulation, and power, all of our relationships can be soul to soul.

A Good Relationship With Yourself

In our society we have many good relationships and many bad relationships and many in-between. Becoming more conscious about your source of love and your expectations in a relationship will help you set up a more balanced flow of love between you and your partner. The real truth is that if you do not have a source of loving energy within, self love, you will never be able to get all the energy you need from another. Love is a vital life force energy. It is a vibration that brings spiritual light into the world. All relationships when open and flowing, are physical expressions of higher energies and help us learn how to love ourselves.

To have a good relationship with others will require having a good relationship with yourself. Imagine that you are an enlightened master. Every moment of your life is one of peace. You never feel empty or lonely. You always feel complete and filled just being who you are at this particular moment of your life. You know your purpose here on earth. You have an intimate relationship with yourself and with your higher source. You love everyone equally because you see that we are all the same, all Gods in process. You feel at one with yourself, your soul, and your life's purpose. What would it be like to have enlightened relationships?

Arriving at a state of enlightenment is the work of our souls. This is not in conflict with any religion. The various religions just provide an understanding of what it means to be enlightened. The real question is: what is a state of enlightenment and how can I get there?

Since the authors cannot make any claim to having reached that state yet, we can only point in a direction to go.

- You reach enlightenment individually and uniquely from all other people. You must find your own path, which may well be within the framework of your religion.

- When you are enlightened, you do not take offense at any event that happens in your life because you know that it is not the event that affects you but your interpretation of the event.

- You feel gratitude at the privilege of living life at every moment.

- You plan for the future but are never attached to your anticipated outcomes for those plans, being free to adapt and adjust to the flow of life.

- You realize that you create your own life: past, present, and future.

- To become enlightened requires exploring yourself, your relationships, your world, and your connection to your soul. You need to learn about all the parts of yourself.

Anytime you are on the path of self exploration and personal spiritual growth, you are on the path of enlightenment. This path will also lead you to more evolved and more loving relationships. **The quality of your relationships with other people depends completely on the quality of your relationship with yourself.**

To have loving relationships and soul relationships, you need to accept and transform any negativity within. Change the darker denser energy of your body, emotions, and mind into higher spiritual light. As you radiate more light from within, more spiritual energy becomes integrated into your life and your outer life will change to match this higher vibration.

Loving yourself is a way to heal old hurts and transform negativity. Loving yourself as much as God loves you is an enlightened state of being. **The quality of your relationship with yourself depends completely on the quality of your relationship with God or your higher source.** Open yourself up to your higher source and allow your body, emotions, and mind to be filled with love. Know that you are a great spiritual being of unlimited loving potential. Open your heart to being loved by your soul.

As we learn to love ourselves and share that higher love with others, we are truly transforming the planet. We are moving into living as our soul's light.

The Playground

Time for some more fun out on the playground. Today we are going to play with our relationships.

Adventure and Explore

As usual, we give you some questions for you to consider alone or for a group to discuss. Remember that there are no right or wrong answers; you don't even have to give one if you feel uncomfortable. Each person simply explores and expresses their own truth, either aloud or to themselves.

Round 1: Identify three energetic qualities you share with your best friend. How are you connected?

Round 2: Are you aware of any people who are draining you energetically? What is the struggle for power that is going on? What is the control drama you are playing out? Why do you let this continue?

Round 3: Is there anyone in your life that you are trying to dominate or control? How often? When? What is going on?

Round 4: Can people know each other soul to soul?

Round 5: Do you have soul relationships in your life? With whom? How do you know?

Create and Play:

We have two games to help you create your reality and play with energy. We hope you enjoy them.

Your Romantic Views

This exercise will help you examine the energies you bring to romantic relationships.

1. Take a piece of paper and put two columns on it, one labeled "ME" and the other labeled "OTHER." Put down the things that you expect to give when in a loving relationship under the "ME" column. Put down the things that you expect to receive in a loving relationship under the "OTHER" column. Push yourself to give at least five things under each column.

2. Look over the expectations and see if there is any imbalance in what you expect to **give** and what you expect to **receive**.

3. How do your expectations limit your possibilities of having a good relationship?

4. Have each person in the group share some of their key expectations and any imbalances they found.

5. Have the group do a short meditation by putting on some quiet background music and sensing how your list feels. What do you sense? Is your list your true definition of a good relationship? Do you expect to give too much? Do you expect to receive too much?

6.   Throw your list away and throw away your expectations, these limit and constrict the natural flow of love.

Having Fun Sending and Receiving Energy

This exercise will help give you a bodily sensation of sending and receiving energy.

1.   Pick a partner. One of you is A and one of you is B. Sit face to face, close enough so that you are almost but not touching. Partner A holds out both hands with palms up. Partner B holds out both hands with palms down over Partner A's hands. Partner B will practice sending energy to Partner A while Partner A practices receiving.

2.   Have everyone in the room get quiet and imagine that they are finding a peaceful, centered place within. Partner B should imagine drawing energy from the earth, up through their heart chakra down through their arms and out the palms of their hands into the palms of Partner A. Partner A should imagine that they are receiving energy from Partner B and flowing this energy into their hands, up their arms, into their heart and then down into the earth. Continue to repeat this exercise until you feel you have created a circuit of energy flowing between the two of you.

3.   Once completed, reverse roles and try again.

4.   Notice if you had any trouble receiving energy. Was it difficult to send energy? How did it feel when you consciously flowed energy through your body?

Touch and Sense

It is time for a meditation on the energy of relationships. During this meditation, focus on letting go of other people's energy. Try to become aware of yourself as a separate energetic being, whole and complete just as you are. You may also want to experiment with letting go of resentments, hatreds, and bad energy that you have hung onto regarding your relationships with others. It is always good to imagine that you are filling your body, emotions, mind, and spirit with loving light.

Explore your inner world. Experience color, light, images, or physical sensations. Know that on any given day, you may feel nothing, or your mind might be filled with the day's chatter. Don't worry about that, just let today's meditation be what it is. Tomorrow's will be different.

The guided meditations are meant to help you to relax, to experience being with your own internal energies, and to have fun. Perhaps you want to listen to the tapes without trying to meditate. Play with the meditations, creating the best experience for you.

The Young Old Masters

CHAPTER 6 ❋ Group Energies

We are born, we live our lives, and we die in the context of a group and its energy. The family, the society, and the world are all a part of our consciousness here on Earth. Our culture shapes the way we think and the way we behave. To change your own individual thinking, you must become aware of the power of group thought. The new age of spiritual awareness is creating the ability to change negative thoughts and be more aware of the cultural thoughtforms (group beliefs) that affect your life.

Our Fun and Games Together

As we gathered this Tuesday night, the group members were quieter than normal. We began to wonder if they sensed ahead of time that this is a tough topic to explore. We started our discussion by looking at the sixth insight in *The Celestine Prophecy*. In the novel, the sixth insight teaches us to look at the parental patterns we adopted as our own and the control dramas we use to gain energy. There are four styles of operating in a life situation: Intimidator, Interrogator, Aloof, and Poor Me or Victim. After doing many years of counseling, Mary pointed out to the group that this is true. People adopt patterns of behavior from the way they were raised and the culture they were raised in. But no one likes to admit that "I intimidate others" or that "I am the victim."

As we interact with our family, friends, lovers, and work associates, people act and react in certain ways. When one person interrogates another, the second person may become withdrawn or aloof in reaction to the strong energy they are feeling. When you play the part of being aloof, not sharing your energy with others, you may create interrogators in your life. Others may feel a need to draw your energy out through intimidation to create a connection.

Each group member identified with a certain type of behavior, a pattern they had developed when interacting with others. We had a long discussion about our parents and their patterns of behavior. As we all began to see that we had indeed adopted or copied a style in reaction to our parents, the energy in the room got very dense and heavy. It was clear we all wanted to be free of behavior patterns that were negative or limiting.

One of the universal psychological questions of our time is how do we really change our behavior? How do you stop being an intimidator? How do you stop being the victim? How do you make a permanent change in yourself by working on the energy level? Talking in our group about creating lasting changes was an opportunity to talk about the importance of healing body, mind, and spirit. Because we exist on all different levels, we must change the energy of negative thoughtforms on all the different levels. This is something these young people had never really thought about before. We spent most of the group session talking about family and group patterns. All the participants agreed it was hard to change yourself even if you want to change.

We used the following example in our discussions. When

you work on the physical level only, you can usually create a small amount of change. For example, if you are a victim around your parents, you can move out of your parents' home. This is creating a physical change. However, the victim mentality usually goes with you to your new apartment. If you work on the mental level and change the thoughts you have about being the victim, this will help change more of your victim behavior, but not all of it. If you are willing to work on the physical, mental, and spiritual level, this can change a pattern completely. Sometimes we must learn about the spiritual aspects of our behavior before we can really be free to live our highest potential.

Connecting with your soul's energy can help you see your patterns of behavior more clearly and make the choice to change. These patterns can be thought of as darker, denser energy. You can change the energy within and transform it into a higher more positive vibration of energy, to create a new pattern of behavior. This energy of negative beliefs often exist in the physical body, in the emotional body, in the mental body and in the spiritual body. Brian then asked, "But how do you heal the soul?".

To heal the soul you have to shift to a higher state of being. Creating a space of higher awareness enables you to connect to your soul's wisdom. On this evening together, to create our sacred space (a soul space), we used smudge and candles. We needed some ritual or focus to help us shift our consciousness.

We began by using a smudge stick. This clump of sage, when burned, creates a gentle smoke like incense. As we smudged the group members, we circled each other, one at a time, with the smoke. We could feel the energy in the room shift to a higher level. The smoke lifted our awareness to a different level and we began to sense some of the spiritual aspects of our behavior. We moved consciously out of the pure physical, opened up the mental energy, and allowed the spiritual energy of our souls to be present. It was powerful to feel the higher energy in the room.

It became clear, as we were finishing our evening together, that we had to create a sacred ceremony that would help release some of the energy of negative behaviors. Since fire and smoke have always been used in spiritual exercises, we decided to create a symbolic cleansing of negative energy with fire.

We gathered together in a circle and each member was given a candle. We turned off the lights and lit the candles one by one around the circle. We asked each person to imagine, as they lit their candle, that they were accepting the light of their soul. We led them on a guided meditation as they stared into their flame of purification.

"Only the light and energy of your higher self can really help clear the past, clear the patterns of behavior that no longer work for who you are becoming in life. You are not your parents, you are not only the son and daughter of someone else. You have come to earth to be your own person, a great spirit, with a purpose and a unique energy to share with the world. You need to be willing to release the old when you no longer need it."

The faces of the group members were bright with the light from their candle and all of them were focused on the flame. We continued to slowly guide them:

"Imagine bringing this flame into your heart, let the flame grow and expand, until you are surrounded by the cleansing energy of fire. Allow the fire to purify and destroy the patterns of dominance, control,

victimization, and separateness. Allow yourself to be changed energetically by the fire of your own purpose that burns in your soul's energy. Release the old patterns so that you can evolve beyond the limits of the physical, emotional, and mental energy. Allow yourself to expand into the full light energy of your soul."

As we finished this exercise, there was a profound peace in the room. The peace that comes from the soul. One by one we blew out the candles and accepted that peace into our hearts. It was an evening of much learning and growth for everyone.

All spiritual masters must question the beliefs of their parents. They must questions the beliefs of their society, their religion, their schooling, and their culture to experience what is the truth. All teach some spiritual truths, but not all we learn comes from the space of love and sacredness. Much of what we adopt as our beliefs comes from fear and fear is a lower energy, it is not the energy of the soul. We ask that you look at what you believe because beliefs govern behavior. If you listen, your spirit will let you know what is true for you.

Listen and Imagine

What Is a Family

A family has become a hard thing to define. Many years ago "the family" was easy to understand. The nuclear family was a father, a mother, and children. The extended family included the grandparents, aunts, uncles, and cousins. There was very little divorce, single moms, gay or lesbian couples, stepdads and the like except in extreme cases. But now families are changing and hard to define.

Many people are nurtured and loved by their nuclear family. But sometimes your "family" becomes the people you are energetically connected to. In the family, we are helped to grow and accepted for who you are. In energy terms a family creates a space of energy for us that holds the light of higher potential. No wonder families are so cherished.

The major roles in a family are just two: those that take care of others and those that are taken care of. The people that fill *both* roles are truly nurtured. People that are taken care of can share the energy of gratitude and appreciation for all of the things done for them. Those who do the care-taking share with the family feelings of competence and pride in what they can provide. When members in a family take both parts to differing degrees at different times, the family has a balanced flow of loving energy.

All types of groupings can constitute and create a family. Can single parent groupings be a family? Of course. Can traditional two parent with children groupings not be families? Of course. Can a group of friends who love and support you be a family? Yes. Family involves daily compassionate energy, nurturing energy, accepting energy, and loving energy.

Sometimes when we are upset or separated from our families, it is difficult to remember that families serve an important and vital role in socializing the infant. When a child is born, some psychologists believe that the child does not know it is separate from its mother. It has grown inside the womb and has only recently left, not recognizing it is not one with the mother. The infant is dependent and like an energetic sponge, absorbing and learning everything from the family.

The young infant has no knowledge of words and no knowledge of the societal structure. It possesses only an energy-sensing system as a way to learn how to live in the family and live in the world. A baby's physical body is equipped with the five senses as well as the ability to sense higher energy flows of people and of nature. But the teachers, the instructors of how they will learn and evolve, are the family.

It is no surprise that children WILL absorb, learn, and adopt the beliefs of their parents, even if the beliefs are negative and detrimental to being more evolved. The family must teach the child and the child must learn from the family. This is not a bad thing, but it can be limiting if all we ever learn or believe is the energy patterns of our families. There is so much more. Even if parents say they want their children to live their own life, often it's not true. Often the parents want their kids to be carbon copies of themselves.

As we evolve into a more aware society and into more spiritually aware families, we have an opportunity to rid ourselves and our children of limiting beliefs. If you ever become a parent, remember the following: **parents with problems raise kids with problems.** One of the hopes we have for you, the reader, is that you begin to understand that you are an energetic being with the wisdom of your soul, before you raise children. When you are more conscious and aware, you can operate from a loving state of being. Being a more loving parent raises the vibration of the whole family. Loving energy creates positive vibrations that can bring the whole earth into the light. Families are an important part of who we are and they give us part of the energy programming of who we will be.

Our Family Energy Connections

We are connected energetically to our family, to our nationality, and to the cultural beliefs of many generations. Mother, father, sister and brother have helped shape who we are and our belief patterns. Families have a special energy vibration and your individual vibration aligns with this group. As we grow, mature, and move away from our family of origin, we take with us that family energy pattern. Sometimes the connections to our mother and father can be imagined as cords or lines of light that connect our spirit to their spirit. These cords can be disconnected in many ways but most people keep some family "ties."

There are spiritual philosophies that state you choose the family you are born into before you come to earth. You want the particular type of energy your family has. Whether or not you can prove this idea, if you do **choose** your family, what have you come to earth to learn from your mother and father? What are you learning from your other family members and from the role you play in this energy group?

Carolyn Myss (pronounced "Mace") has written extensively in her book, *Anatomy of a Spirit,* about the energy system that we are and about our energetic connections to our family, society, and culture. She calls the primary group our "tribe." These connections that we are born into affect our energy supply and our perception of our own power. People cannot heal completely without personal power, in other words, the energy of the spirit. It becomes important as we grow and evolve to look at our energetic connection to our family and how this relates to aligning the energy of your body, mind, and spirit. For example, if you have adopted a family belief that says you will "fail" or you are "not good enough," it will become necessary to unplug from the energy of that family belief, in order to succeed. Myss states that we lose power when part of our energy system is plugged into negative beliefs coming from the tribe, the family, the marriage, or any other group or system.

Families are important for our growth and development here on earth. Families teach us how to love, connect with others, and live successfully in our society. It is not important to disconnect completely from your family to become your own person. However, it is important to make a distinction between your own truth and family truths that can limit your potential. No families are perfect, no parents are perfect, no schools are perfect, but these systems give us a start on our life's path. To reach our full potential, we must take full responsibility for what we do with the rest of our life. The important thing about spiritual growth work is that you begin to learn, through your soul connection, that you are the creator of your life. You can unplug your energy circuits from the tribe and let your spirit speak to you about the meaning of your life.

Peer Groups

We are not only born into a family, we are also born into a particular point in time. Energetically, we are born into a particular peer group. The energy of people born in the 1940's is different from the energy of individuals born in the1980's. We are raised in a certain generation that has its own particular energy, a peer group vibration. There was a generation that went through World War II together, the generation that went through the 60's together and the present generation of young adults who may be categorized as the X,Y, or Z generation, or as Pepsi says, "Generation Next." Beliefs and truths and even awareness of spiritual energy are different as we move through time. There is no doubt that one's peer group is very important. If we tried to write this book in the 1700's, that peer group might be inclined to burn us at the stake, rather than buy this book. The present generation is more open to new ideas, so, certain thoughts, concepts, and beliefs can be presented that may not have been accepted before this time.

It could be said that each generation brings in a new energy. Especially in our present time, the energy of a spiritual evolution (outside of standard religious structure) is now more present in society. Take a look at your peers. What new beliefs do they bring with them? Possibly beliefs that have never been on the planet before such as traveling on the Internet and making world connections. Certainly our grandmothers never believed this would be possible when they were young. Could your generation be the ones who truly connect with the soul and live a more energized life? Could you link soul to soul to enhance each others lives? Could you learn how to transmit spiritual energy so the whole planet moves in a more positive direction?

Every "new" generation is criticized for thinking differently, for moving beyond the old limiting beliefs of its mothers and fathers. But we believe this questioning of the old must happen to bring in the new. Each generation has a special role to play in helping the planet evolve and change into a higher way of life, a life where each person on the planet is empowered to be a great soul and have all their earthly needs met. We do not know yet if this will happen quickly or will take many more generations, but we do know that you and your friends have a special role to play in the future of Mother Earth. It is time now to begin asking as a group, a peer group, a new energy group, what have we come here to do? In asking these questions of your higher self, guidance will come to help you and your peers discover the answers.

Young people have been criticized for being too violent, for teenage pregnancies, for drug use, for speaking out. These "problems" do contain much negative energy. But these are also opportunities to learn how to choose a higher way. It is not unusual for mankind to experience the negative before choosing a more positive way of life. We believe there is a reason for everything. It is up to you to see the way in which negative events are educating you and your generation.

More than any one thing, the present young generation seems freer than generations before. Free to connect to each other outside of racial and ethnic lines. Free to express sexuality. Free to think that anything is possible. Is the energetic quality of freedom from barriers and rules what is necessary to evolve spiritually? In some ways yes, freeing ourselves from mental, emotional, and spiritual limitations is a part of becoming a fully connected body, mind, and spirit. Maybe your generation is the one to move beyond the boundaries of the "little self" and fully explore the vast energy of the soul and higher dimensions. It feels like we are all being asked to move in that direction.

Societal Groups

It's easy to think of society as THEM. It is a little more difficult to think of society as US. Who is the society? It is each one of us, all put together. Who is the government? That's us again. Who is the IRS? Our neighbors and ourselves. Who was the thief that robbed the jewelry store? Our neighbors and ourselves. How can the society and government have so many things we do not like in it if it is somehow the summation of all of us individuals? Like it or not, we are part of a large, interconnected group energy called a society or a culture.

Gigantic social structures are a complete reflection of our current mass consciousness. In other words, they are mass thoughtforms. They are collective energy grids that guide the way people behave and think in any society. As a group we think, feel, and act in similar ways through our shared vibration. A society is a collective consciousness that participates in the same energy, usually unconsciously. A mass thoughtform is a summation of energy across a number of individuals.

There were societies that used to think the world was flat and this mass thoughtform did not make it right. The men and women of the human race used to think that women didn't need to participate during a vote on an important issue, but that mass belief of the past doesn't make it right for today. Many societal beliefs exist that are not necessarily good or right, but even rigid mass thoughtforms change over time. As we bring more spiritual light into our reality, we will question our rigid beliefs.

Evolving yourself or evolving a society is not a comfortable or easy thing. But as we bring more energy to the planet, this light floods society and begins to loosen rigid thoughts creating openings for higher thoughtforms. Society, like the family, exists to keep order energetically among all the different people living on earth. As the individual changes, the family changes, and the society changes. This evolution brings new thought, new awareness, and new possibilities to the world. The role of society itself will change and grow as we grow energetically.

Seeking Your Truth

To become the master of your own life you have to examine the beliefs adopted from your parents, your peers, your society, and your culture and decide what is true for you. Some parental, peer, and societal beliefs are good ones. Some may not match the vibration of who you are. You have a choice of which to use.

There is an energy in your truth. The difficulty one always has is knowing what the truth is for you. It is OK to adopt the beliefs of your parents, your peers, or your society for issues that you have not had time to examine yourself. But as you become more in tune with who you are, when you start to behave and believe in ways that are not true for you, you will notice an uneasy feeling arise. This is your signal that you are not living your own truth but the truth of someone else. You need to go within and find out what your truth is and live it.

As you move into living your truth every day it will affect your past, your present, and your future. It will change your past, truly change it. The important thing about your past is not the actual events that occurred. The important thing is how you interpreted those events. Yes, you can go back and change how you choose to interpret your past life events and their effect on you.

In your present, while you are in the middle of the experience of this moment, you can put all of your history aside. You can forget what your society told you, you can forget what your peers told you, you can forget what your parents told you. You can even, honestly, forget what you tell yourself. You are never in the same place twice in your life, no matter what you might feel like. So just because something has happened in a certain way for the last 100 times does not mean it will occur that way the next time. When you put away your history, you can live in the moment and truly experience your experience.

For your future, you can understand how fragile any image you have of the future truly is. An image of the future is what you expect to happen in the time to come. But that expectation is no more real than the expectations and beliefs of parents, peers, and society. Do not be bound by such things. Be ready to abandon them easily.

Christ and other great religious figures have performed miracles. Christ said "Greater things than I have done you can do also." If the mass thoughtform says that water is not the same as wine, maybe we all are stuck without miracles. But when someone arrives with the energy and love of God and knows that "drinking water is not wine" is just a belief like thinking the world is flat, suddenly the water can turn into wine and a wedding celebration can continue.

How do your beliefs, wherever they came from, limit you? What is your truth about yourself and your life? As you get clearer about your own beliefs and the higher meaning of your life, you will find yourself **living your truth.** Living your truth is a very high state of being. It is living in the energy of your highest potential. It is living as your soul.

This is our hope for you, to know, experience, and live your highest truth.

The Playground

Time for some more fun out on the playground. Today we are going to go to play with the groups in our life - the family groups, the peer groups, and the societal groups.

Adventure and Explore

We give some questions here for you to consider alone or for a group to discuss. There are no right or wrong answers; you don't even have to give one if you feel uncomfortable. Each person should explore and express their own truth, either aloud or to themselves.

Round 1: To whom do you have the strongest energetic tie in your family? Mother? Father? Sister? Brother? Grandparents? Aunt? Uncle? Cousin?

Round 2: What are some of the positive and negative energy attributes you got from your family?

Round 3: What are some of the ways in which you could "unplug" from family beliefs that limit you?

Round 4: Why do you think you were born into your family? Your culture? Your particular society?

Round 5: What special qualities does your generation bring to earth?

Round 6: How is the vibration of love expressed through your peer group?

Round 7: What special higher awareness do you have that your parents don't have?

Round 8: How is creative energy expressed through your peer group?

Create and Play:

We have two games to help you create your reality and do energy play with each other. We hope you enjoy them.

Mass Thoughtforms and You

This exercise will help you look at how mass thoughtforms or beliefs affect you.

1. On a piece of paper, have everyone in the room write down a positive and a negative belief that they have. For example, positive beliefs might be, "Anyone can get a good job if they believe in themselves," or "My family is great at..." Examples of negative beliefs are, "People cannot be trusted" or "The stock market is bound to crash." Don't forget about beliefs regarding

relationships, family, society, religion, or other important aspects of your life.

2. Share your beliefs with the group and have a discussion about how societal, family, and personal beliefs affect you. Discuss how people become indoctrinated in thinking a certain way. Identify mass thoughtforms that affect all of us, such as, "There will always be wars" or "There is not enough for everyone." What would happen if you stopped agreeing with a mass thoughtform? How could you spend the energy of your thoughts differently?

3. Identify for yourself a negative belief that you have adopted from your family or culture. Don't be embarrassed, we all have them. Write it on a piece of paper. Give it to the person on your left. Go around the room and have each person read the belief and lead a discussion about transforming this belief into a higher thoughtform. How can this belief be transformed into a more positive energy?

Freeing Your Energy

1. Identify some belief or pattern of thinking or a negative aspect of your self image that you would like to change. Picture in your mind the way in which the energy in this belief has tied you up.

2. Each person in the room should take a candle. Set the energy in the room by putting on some background meditation music. Imagine that you are going to cleanse with fire your connection to this belief.

Imagine that your intention is to sever this tie. Cut the cords. Unplug your energy from this belief.

3.   Before you light your candle, become focused and centered on the higher energy available in the room. Place a lit candle in the center of the circle. One person lights their candle from this center light and then passes the flame around the circle, each person giving the fire to the person next to them.

4.   As you stare into the flame, allow yourself to blend with that light. This light becomes the light of freedom. The light of separating from energies that you no longer want or need. Keep imagining that you are freeing yourself from the energetic ties of the old beliefs until you feel it in your heart.

5.   When you are complete, extinguish your candle.

6.   Join in a group discussion about what you sensed during this exercise. Consider how you can repeat this exercise for other issues that bind you.

Touch and Sense

There are thoughts and beliefs that you have adopted in your life from others without awareness. Some of them are negative or limiting. Meditation is a good way to work on changing limiting thoughts, getting new insights, and expanding your power to manage your life. As you grow spiritually, you will be working on creating new thoughtforms for yourself based on your life experiences.

So it is time for another meditation journey. Get yourself in a comfortable physical position. Be ready to play a tape in its entirety, which takes about 30 minutes. Try to find a time and space when you will not be interrupted. Remember to turn off the phone and the pagers. Use whatever rituals will help prepare a quiet inner space.

Explore your inner world. Experience color, light, images, or physical sensations. Every day is different in meditation. Don't worry about it, just let today's meditation be what it is. Tomorrow's will be different.

If you do not enjoy meditating or don't want to meditate, then don't. Just listening to the tapes without trying to meditate will give you much benefit.

The Young Old Masters

CHAPTER 7 ✳ Connecting With Higher Energies

Your life is not difficult or easy, good or bad, fulfilling or pointless. It just is. What makes it feel like all of these things is the kind of energy you hold within yourself. You can learn to change your internal energy and your attitude toward yourself and your life. You can raise your vibration, independently of the relationships you are in and independently of the society in which you live. You can do this by connecting to your soul or higher self and accessing its energy. There is a higher community of light that loves you, cares about you, and wants to support you in your own growth and the growth and evolution of all mankind. So connecting to the higher energies is a way for you to know this more directly. There is also an energy of peace, joy, and bliss that can only be found in the higher realms. When you meditate and connect with the higher energies, you can bring this peace, joy, and bliss into your own life.

Our Fun and Games Together

In every life, there are those special evenings when you are not expecting anything in particular, but the Universe has something special in mind. As we gathered for our last class, the energy in the room was electric. Chris said to Mary that we ought to have the young people try some channeling. Mary's first thought was, "Are you crazy?" But since the whole group had been an experiment, she changed her mind and said, "Let's try it." What is that special force that gives us a creative idea to work on? We began by asking if anyone had any coincidences to report and happily shared a few things with the group.

We told the group members that we were going to ask each one of them to lead a meditation and speak a journey from their heart. Of course, they were not sure they could do it but were willing to try. To help these young people get into a higher space, we decided to "smudge" each person individually. Chris is quite masterful at setting the energy in the room and lit the sage smudge stick. One by one each member stood in the center of our circle and he slowly and purposely cleared their energy with the smoke.

As he surrounded them with the smoke, he gently directed each of them to imagine they are connecting with their higher self. *"Imagine the energy of your soul is blending with your physical body and the energy of your higher self is opening your heart."* Chris and Mary knew these young people had the wisdom of their soul within and both held the vision that they could speak from the energy of their higher self. Allowing your soul to speak through you is a type of channeling. It is powerful for the group to hear and powerful for the individual to speak.

The room became peaceful, the higher energies were present, and the background music helped us get into a meditative state. This clearing with smoke had a way of shifting the energy from our everyday awareness to a sacred energy space. We could feel the presence of soul energy in the room. Mary began the journey, leading the members into a connection with their higher selves and called on each member, one at a time, to speak their wisdom from the heart. It was not the words that were spoken that made this special, it was the presence of each person's light that we could actually feel. Each was different, each was pure and loving, each had the power of God's light flowing through the words they spoke. It was an amazing event in our group and an evening we will not forget.

As we returned to present time and reality and left the space of our higher self in the higher dimensions, there was a profound state of peace in each one of us. This group of young people had channeled their higher selves. The interesting thing about experiencing the higher energies is that it is different for each person. Some people see energy patterns, some people feel waves or vibrations, others sense the energy in a combined way. Each member could sense the presence of their higher self or their soul as they channeled a meditation journey. We looked at them and said, "Do you realize that you just lead your first meditation!"

We shared our experiences and each person liked something different about the other persons' journey. We found our experiences hard to explain because words are so limiting. When you feel yourself walking through a magical forest that has energy glowing off of every tree, it is quite a different experience than reading about it. There were such strong feelings of self confidence and accomplishment as we completed the group that night. We gathered together in one large group hug.

After that experience, it was so clear that the soul is the larger part of ourselves, the part that knows anything is possible. It is only the little physical self that has doubt and fear. When you step outside of the small self, you join with the higher you and the higher flow. When the higher you is present, spiritual light flows through the physical body, emotional body, and the mental body and this is a great feeling.

Listen and Imagine

Meditation

The concept of meditation has many strange connotations in our world. Many people probably imagine some type of Buddhist monk sitting in austere surroundings, in lotus position, chanting the "Ohm." Others picture some type of hippie commune with incense in the air and psychedelic pictures on the wall. Though either of these images is sometimes true, the fact of the matter is that many ordinary people all over the world sit in an easy chair, play some light music in the background, close their eyes, and spend 20 to 30 minutes meditating a number of times each week, some a couple of times every day. The actual impact of meditation is well known, highly positive, and scientifically documented in study after study.

One of the first popular books to examine meditation was *The Relaxation Response*. It examined the impact of meditation on people's lives. It documented substantial medical benefits (e.g., reduction of high blood pressure), personal benefits (e.g., stress reduction), and societal benefits (e.g., meditators are active members of society that get things done).

Meditation connects your ego to your higher self, your soul. It connects people together. *"Whenever two or more of you are gathered in my name, there is love,"* came from a song often played at weddings but originated in the Bible. Jesus knew that something special happened when people came together to reflect on his teachings and connected to their spiritual energy.

Energetically, consider the following image. Your soul came into this world, into this loud and sensory filled world. The dense energies of this world are just plain loud. The images of light flood your eyes with each waking moment. The vibrations of sound touch your ears and even your skin, demanding attention. Your taste and smell are highly activated every time you sit down to eat. And, of course, your sense of touch provides you with the greatest feelings of nurturance and love. Literally billions of nerves are firing in your body at any moment, receiving inputs from outside the body, from inside the body, directing muscles to perform their function. Somewhere, amid all this riot of pulsing energy, is the energy of your soul, the energy of you.

With the loud noises of this world shouting at you from every direction, it is hard to hear the energy of your soul, the inner voice of who you really are. That is what meditation lets us do.

The real purpose of meditation is to enter into a state of being in which we turn down the volume of the outside world. Generally, you don't turn it off. You can still hear the phone ring, the gentle music in the background, the snoring of someone who slipped from meditation into sleep. But with the volume of this world turned down, we have an opportunity to listen to the inner voice within us all. That inner voice has a higher wisdom that is not fooled by all the confusion of this world.

However you choose to meditate, remember a couple of pointers. First, every meditation experience is different. Many people, at some time or another, have a mystical experience during meditation only to have the next meditation be a difficult one with frequent distractions. Let each meditation be what it is. There is no such thing as a wrong meditation experience. You can't do anything that will hurt yourself or take you to some place you should not be.

Different people choose to meditate in different ways. Always choose the way that feels most effective to you. Feel free to experiment with what creates deeper meditations for you and brings you into feelings of inner peace. Some of the variations include:

- Meditate in silence, repeating the universal mantra "Ohm" or your own personal tone or mantra.
- Meditate following a guided meditation tape or journey.
- Meditate by trying to keep your mind completely clear of all thoughts, creating "no thought" and inner silence.
- Meditate trying to affirm a particular image of your life, creating a picture or visualization of what you want for your life.
- Connect with God or a religious figure and let your meditation be a prayer.

Secondly, don't worry about falling asleep. Many people lead lives so busy that they try to meditate after a long and trying day. They start the meditation only to find themselves waking up from sleep sometime later. In many ways, meditation is exactly about getting ever closer to the sleep mode of consciousness without going into it. With that in mind, it's not surprising that sometimes we slide over the edge. Eventually you will want to maintain that meditative state between wakefulness and sleep.

Finally, don't worry about not maintaining your meditation goals. Everyone's life is complex. It would be wonderful if you could manage to meditate for twenty minutes on rising and for another twenty minutes in the evening. But if you can only find a few times a week to do it, you will still benefit from the effort. Meditation is for you. It is a time of self discovery. Enjoy the feelings of it and know you are moving yourself closer to the divine with each meditation you do.

Creating a Sacred Space in Your Life

We have been educating you about energy principles and the fact that you are an energy being. To create inner peace, you need to look at outer peace or lack of peace in your life. Why is peace so important anyway? From a space of peace, your soul can speak to you. When you are peaceful, creativity flows and you can know the highest path for your life. This is not to say that insights don't come when you are not peaceful. Rather, clearer insights and more spiritual light are available from a peaceful, centered state.

Being centered may be thought of as the small you, the physical body, sitting in the center of a vast sphere of your soul's light. When you are centered, your mind is focused on your self and your own energy. Your emotions are calm and flowing. Being centered is a state of peace, inner focus, and higher awareness all at the same time. It is difficult to know if you are peaceful or not until you try to center yourself.

When you are trying to create a sacred, peaceful space for yourself, the first thing you may notice is how much the mind is racing through many thoughts and ideas. Creating a quiet mind is a skill to be learned and practiced. In fact, as you quiet the outer body, you may notice the inner you is in turmoil. Emotions are energy, thoughts are energy, and your physical body is energy. At any given moment in time, one or all three systems are active and not peaceful. We absorb energy from our outer world and we are energy in our inner world. The soul, however, is active and peaceful at the same time.

One thing that happens to people as they become spiritually aware is that they also become aware of their environment. You may feel inclined to change the energy in your bedroom, office, car, or household. As you gain more inner peace, you may want your outer environment to change and reflect that peace. Sometimes jobs and certain relationships become intolerable energetically. You may feel drawn to change your outer world as you change on the inside. Making changes in your life that are for your highest good is a positive thing, but not always comfortable.

We encourage you to create some sacredness in your life. Create a light-filled environment to live in. Connect with the beautiful things in life and feed your soul. Make time to get quiet and learn more about your inner self. When you know yourself and you know what enhances your energy, you can create a life that flows. Creating a sacred space means honoring and loving yourself. Create love, light, and beauty in your outer environment and learn how to have love, light, and beauty on the inside too. This is the kind of human existence your soul wants for you.

The Gridwork of Light: Your Soul's Playground

When you view yourself from an energetic perspective, many life experiences become clearer. You are four major types of energy, all interacting with each other, each type having its own particular vibration at every moment in time. As you read this book, you are activating at least some of your mental energies and, if the words touch your heart, your emotional or even spiritual vibration may rise as well. The goal is to raise your vibration in each of the four areas and do it in a manner that keeps them balanced.

When we raise our vibration, we can know and understand our connection to all other human beings, animals, plants, Mother Earth, and the spiritual community of higher beings. Our spiritual energies do connect us with others. In fact, one way of picturing this is imagining large conduits of spiritual power stretching across the world. These conduits connect together every person with every other person on the planet. These conduits are energetic and real and have been called the Gridwork of Light by some. Some people see and feel them when they meditate or get into a state of higher consciousness.

It brings to mind one of the old fashioned trolley cars with the network of wires running above the street. Any given trolley car had a connector that rose high into the air and touched this gridwork of power. Only when the connector touched the grid of power did the car run most efficiently. Such is the spiritual Gridwork of Light, a gridwork filled with the energy of life. When we connect to the spiritual gridwork, our personal power and light is increased and we are then our most efficient. We can tap into and use the spiritual gridwork to become more connected to our soul's light. It contains infinite energy and has free access for all.

An individual person connected to this gridwork becomes a complex system for relaying power and transmitting light. The source for the power is the gridwork itself, although the individual is not always aware that this is true. The power from the gridwork keeps coming; new power, more power, all the time. So we have to be sure to do something with all that energy, otherwise our physical system starts to overload.

For the individual's system to work properly, the energy coming from the gridwork needs to flow in all of the different energy centers of the body, with a free exchange of energy, with a free flow of energy, and with a free transformation of energy. Sometimes, the individual can do things to constrict energy flow. The constriction occurs because the individual forgets that the supply of energy is truly unlimited, and, instead, begins to believe that the energy may run out. In a reaction to this improper belief, the individual tries to restrict the flow of energy so that not as much is "needed" or the individual tries to hoard energy so if the supply is cut off, they will have a supply to back themselves up. That is where all of the pains in our world come from. We do not trust that the infinite wisdom and joy of the divine is available to us at every moment. Instead we feel that we are limited. We will be cut off. We start to hoard energy which makes us view ourselves in competition with other people. It makes us want to steal energy from other people.

The only thing we really want is to feel good. The only way we can really feel good is to have no restrictions of flow in our energy bodies. One way to have unrestricted energy flows is to discard our ideas about limitation. If we throw away the images that say there is not enough. If we trust that light and energy is always available, equally and without judgment, from the Gridwork of Light. We can know there is nothing to fear and all we need will be provided by the Higher Communities of Light.

The Urge to Know Your Soul

It seems as if we are all on the road to seeking the truth of who we are. This "truth" about the soul and the "truth" about the universe is the foundation of many religions, groups, and sects participating in many forms of worship. It is difficult to imagine that we are all seeking the same God, the same "truth." Some would say that if you take away religion, people would have no faith in God, but how can this be true when many devout spiritual people do not align with any particular religion? We believe there are many paths to the one source and the urge for any individual to find their divinity, the God within, will continue on and on.

The Islam religion has a particular kind of practitioner, a kind of holy person called a Sufi. They have a word that describes the basic human urge to find mystical experiences in life. The word is Anguruzuminabstafil. That word comes from the following story:

> *Four men were traveling together, a Persian, a Turk, an Arab, and a Greek. At one particular moment in their travels, they had run out of funds and had began an argument about spending their last coin.*
>
> *The Persian said, "I want to buy angur."*
>
> *The Turk said, "We cannot waste money on that! We must buy uzum."*
>
> *"No," said the Arab, "I feel we must purchase inab."*

To which the Greek replied, "Never! We must have stafil."

A passing stranger heard their argument and approached the men. "Give me your one coin and I will make you all happy," he said.

After much discussion, they decided to trust him. The stranger crossed the town square to a fruit peddler and bought four small bunches of grapes with the coin and returned the grapes to the men.

"Perfect!" cried the Persian, "My angur!"

"Oh!" said the Turk, "That is what we call uzum."

"And, in my language, it is inab," responded the Arab.

"What tasty stafil," finished the Greek.

The disharmony was caused because they did not understand each other. We all have an urge to know our soul, to know our God. Knowing God is a personal and individual process. This knowing will be described differently in different cultures and through different religious beliefs.

This Sufi story emphasizes that we all feel the need to connect to our source, our God, our life. We each have experiences about trying to make this connection that are, quite literally, beyond words. Chris knows a man, a devout Christian, who prays frequently every day to God but will not let his children meditate. Is this a true distinction or are prayer and meditation the same thing? We do not know. The words we use to try and describe the two things are so inadequate that we cannot tell if they are the same or different.

The Islam religion has a meditative mantra that says "There is no God but God." It does ring true that, no matter what we or you or anyone else might think about God and how the universe is set up, it is what it is. There is a truth. Can we, apparently limited beings in this small world, understand an infinite God?

A phrase often used in personal growth work is "Understanding is the booby prize." We are complete beings composed of many kinds of energy – the intellectual energy of understanding is only one type and should not be the total focus of our life. Do we really need to understand life to love it and enjoy it, no matter what it brings? For us, the answer is definitely no.

Enjoy life. Remember another Sufi saying: "Be in this world but not of this world." Two small prepositions, "in" and "of", say so much. Be present to this life, fully engaged, savoring every moment. Do this while remembering that you are truly connected to your soul and part of a much greater reality. You **are** connected to an energy force greater than yourself even if you do not realize this truth.

Remember You are a Soul

Throughout this chapter we are talking about connecting with higher energies. The soul may be thought of as your energy field that connects you to everything else on earth, in the universe, and in the higher dimensions of the soul plane. Your soul is your "best friend." Your soul is wise. Your soul is the energy of love, healing, grace, power, evolution, creativity, higher potential, connection, compassion, joy, intuitiveness, inventiveness, wonder, and peace. The soul is your source of life force energy while you are here on earth.

We are all in the process of learning about soul connection and the meaning of our spiritual energy. We want you to explore your soul. Meditation is a very good way to blend with your soul's energy and be a student of spirituality. When we asked our group members to blend with their soul's light and speak from their higher self, all the participants were changed by that experience. It will be hard for anyone in our group to deny they have a soul, because they have experienced it for themselves.

When we come to earth in a physical incarnation, we feel separate from our soul but, in reality, just like a best friend, our soul is always there. Talk to your soul and listen for the answers. Allow yourself to be led through your life, opening to learning and spiritual growth. In *The Celestine Prophecy,* the book begins and ends with the idea that if we allow our higher self to guide us through coincidences, we will uncover spiritual truths and expand our consciousness. We will grow to know our soul and experience the greater meaning of our life.

The best way to describe experiencing the soul or higher self is to say you can feel a profound love. Not just a good feeling of love, but a love that is compassionate, deep, lasting, and eternal. A love that has power and healing. When you connect with your soul you can suddenly know things that are "not knowable." You will probably increase your psychic abilities and will be able to read and sense energy. As more and more people around the planet learn ways to connect with their soul, we are bringing more light to the world. As you open to more of your soul's energy within, you radiate that higher vibration out. This process of radiating more and more light is what is creating more spiritual energy here on earth.

You and your soul's energy are an important part of the evolution of the planet. We believe if you are reading this book, you have an important part to play in the spiritual awakening of this universe. Allow your "best friend" to show you your highest path. Allow all the problems and situations you go through in life to be a part of your learning. Your soul brings you the things that you must learn in order to evolve and grow. But do not use your lessons as a way to degrade or beat yourself up. Your soul, just like your best friend, believes in you and the wisdom, power, and love you have within.

Through our souls we are connected to the higher communities of light. We are connected to the Angels, the Guides, the Ascended Masters, and Great Beings of Light. You don't have to believe this to be connected to your soul. You may think of the higher realm or heaven as God. Whatever you call your higher source, it is an energy presence greater than yourself.

Becoming enlightened means fully connecting with your soul's energy, grace, and understanding. Your soul is your connection to everything else in the universe. There is a basic spiritual truth about growing to enlightenment that we believe. You cannot be evil, hateful, mean, or a source of negative energy for the world and fully connect to your soul's light at the same time. The soul is connected to God and connected to all other souls and when you "hurt" others you are hurting yourself through this connection. **This is not the way of the soul.** Your higher self is the energy of love and spiritual light. You have come to earth and will experience denser and lower energies. But you have **not** come here to **be** these lower energies. You have come to evolve them to a higher vibration. This is what your soul wants for you.

Embrace your soul, your "best friend," and feel the higher vibrations. Allow higher love to flow through you and onto every part of your life. If enough people live in this way, we will have a peaceful, clean, safe, and loving planet. We will know the Divine Plan for humanity and the part we play in this plan. The soul knows your true purpose and will guide you. When you are able to be more connected, body, mind, and spirit, living is joyful and life is an adventure. The pieces of the puzzle will fit together one by one just like the journey evolved in *The Celestine Prophecy*. Opening to receive your soul's light is a way of honoring yourself and making your life a sacred journey.

The Playground

Time for some more fun out on the playground. Today we are going to go to play with the higher energies available to each of us in life.

Adventure and Explore

We give some questions here for you to consider alone or for a group to discuss. There are no right or wrong answers; you don't even have to give one if you feel uncomfortable. Each person should explore and express their own truth, either aloud or to themselves.

Round 1: If you had to explain to someone else what your soul looked like, how would you describe your soul?

Round 2: When you meditate, or pray, or contemplate, how do you know you are connecting with a higher source?

Round 3: Throughout history, people have killed and destroyed in "God's name." What do you think about this?

Round 4: Natural disasters occur, like famines, floods, hurricanes and earthquakes. Is God responsible for these?

Round 5: How would the world be different if we lived in the energy of love?

Round 6: Can you really connect to the higher energies without opening to God's love?

Round 7: Do you love yourself?

Create and Play:

We have two games to help you experience higher energies directly. We hope you enjoy them.

Transmitting Love

The purpose of this exercise is to have people experience connecting with higher energies and noticing their connections to others. You should do this exercise more than once. Do it once with someone you know well and again with someone new to you. Notice the differences in your experience.

Put on some meditative music, light a candle, turn down the lights, keep your clothes on, and partner up in groups of two.

In each group, let one person be partner A and the other be partner B. Sit face to face and give yourselves a few minutes to become quiet, calm, and peaceful. Close your eyes and imagine as a partnership that you are surrounding yourselves with higher spiritual energy. You might imagine that you are creating a cocoon of light around the two of you. Some people picture this as white light, some as beautiful iridescent colors.

Partner A will begin be imagining that they are connecting to their higher self and sending spiritual love from their heart center to the heart center of partner B. Continue to transmit loving energy for a few minutes. Notice your feelings as the person transmitting the light and as the person receiving the light.

Switch roles and partner B focuses on transmitting loving energy from their heart center to the heart center of partner A.

When you complete this exercise, sit quietly a few moments and collect your thoughts. Share your impressions and experiences of the energy with each other.

Channeling Your Higher Guidance

This exercise can be one of the most exciting things you've ever done. It helps you try to connect, consciously, with your own higher guidance. Channeling is a natural skill. People get "intuitions" and "guidance" all the time. Let this group experience be a easy, relaxed, and natural thing for you to try. Do not worry about being "right" or "wrong," but just try to give your honest and heartfelt truths.

Sometimes our souls speak to us in pictures or colors or energy feelings rather than in words. Feel free to share the pictures you receive in your mind's eye as you do this exercise.

Again, this exercise works best when people are in a meditative environment. Pair up with someone and choose a partner A and a partner B. Partner A will think of a problem or situation about which they would like more guidance. Partner B will be the one channeling the higher wisdom.

Sit quietly together and imagine that you are creating a sacred space together. As partner A gets quiet and looks at the problem or situation, partner A should create a question to partner B. When ready, partner A will tell partner B what the question is.

Prior to answering the question, some people feel a subtle energy change or they have a thought that is clear that they should share. The most important thing for partner B to do is to let go of their fears and relax, focusing on the question that has been presented to them. Share ideas, impressions, energies, colors, or whatever comes into their consciousness regarding the question asked by partner A.

This exercise can be repeated any time you wish, between you and anyone you feel drawn to work with. A fascinating variation on the exercise is to have the partner doing the channeling to channel before hearing the problem or issue raised by the other partner. The guidance of higher energies need not wait for human thought processes. It is always available.

This is also a fun exercise to try as a group. The group sets up a meditative energy for all to share, and then each individual will silently channel information for themselves. Some people keep notebooks nearby as they meditate, as often they will get higher insights and guidance during meditation.

Touch and Sense

As you continue to practice meditation, you begin to realize that meditation is actually the reconnection to the higher energies of life. Just for fun, try to connect to a spirit guide or an angel. See if you can sense the difference between your own soul's energy and the energies of a higher being. Can you sense the soul of a friend?

Meditation is simple. You are going to listen to a guided meditation journey. Get in a comfortable position, sitting or lying quietly. Be ready to play a tape in its entirety, which takes about 30 minutes. Try to find a time and space when you will not be interrupted. Turn off the phone and the pagers. Light a candle, play background music, or follow whatever ritual that will help you prepare a quiet inner space.

Explore your inner world. Experience color, light, images, or physical sensations. Know that on any given day, you may feel nothing, or your mind might be filled with the day's chatter. Don't worry about that, just let today's meditation be what it is. Tomorrow's will be different.

Guided meditations are meant to help you to relax, to experience being with your own internal energies and to have fun. Perhaps you want to listen to the tapes without trying to meditate. Play with the meditations, creating the best experience for you.

CHAPTER 8 — Using Energy in Your Life

Using spiritual energies to expand your life is an individual and creative process. Each person must explore for themselves how to do this. Calling on your higher self to help you transform a situation in your life works. You don't have to understand what you are doing or have any kind of deep spiritual beliefs, it still works. Try it! We have all found, through trial and error, that adding spiritual light to a specific situation in our life, changes it for the better. The best way to know yourself as an energetic being and to understand how focusing on spiritual energy can affect your life is to see how other people use energy and light.

Listen and Imagine

We learn and grow through sharing our thoughts and insights and energy with each other. We asked the group members to answer the questions presented in this chapter, sharing with you their answers from a spiritual perspective. As you explore the following questions, remember there are an infinite number of ways to use spiritual energy in life. As you face choices, problems, and relationship struggles, ask for solutions from a higher state of being. Ask your soul. You can learn to live in a higher flow.

What is it like to have an energetic connection to another person or place?

Todd

The best way I can describe an energetic connection is that it is like a sense that I am in the right place at the right time. It is often as if I am overcome with a positive wave of emotion or euphoria. It makes me feel like I am content with my life at that instant. I wish I could say that these experiences are easy to hang on to and that I am perpetually content with the world, but I often find myself frustrated with my inability to hang on to positive energetic experiences or connections. I have found that through energetic awareness I have been able to open myself more to these experiences. This has enabled me to both enjoy these moments more and hold onto the positive energy that is given to me by connections to people or places.

Brian

Energetic connections to people seem to be more like soul connections rather than energy connections. Sometimes when I meet someone, I will notice them more than others. They will stick in my mind or we will start off getting along extraordinarily well. Those people often end up being the ones I am energetically connected to. I feel like that connection means that I have something to learn or many things to learn from that person. They might not know it, and I never know how or what I will learn, but I always get something profound out of the relationship. I believe that in connected relationships, they get something important out of it as well. Being in an energetically connected relationship is wonderful. I can just look into the person's eyes and know. Know what? No, just know. Also these relationships usually contain more coincidences than others, which shows me that having that person in my life is right for me at the time. People I feel connected to are more aligned with me energetically and always seem to understand me better than those I don't feel connected to. I like to have as many deeper relationships like this as I can. They seem more real and give me more of a taste for life.

Places are much different than people in terms of energetic connections. I usually feel comfortable around the place I like. If I have never been somewhere before, I will feel like everything is much more vivid and clear. However, when I visited the Swiss Alps, I discovered I do have an energetic connection to that part of the world. I felt very alive in that place.

Chris

Having an energetic connection to another person or place is something that happens automatically for me. I couldn't stop it if I tried. Sometimes, like with a couple of close friends of mine, both recent friends, I felt comfortable and at home with them the moment we met. It was like I could feel their open heart. My heart said, "Yeah!" and popped right open itself and connected to these people that I had never met before. Our connection to each other remains. Many times I've met someone and I knew we just weren't going to get along, the feeling was very negative. I don't know, maybe that sounds kind of judgmental, but I've found that it is far better for me to trust these reactions than not. Maybe it's just acknowledging that I do care about the energy

I surround myself with, and I want some kinds near and some kinds kept far away. I choose to be in more positive relationships.

Meg

For me, I get the feeling of unconditional love. I realize I can connect with that place or thing whenever I feel the need to. An energetic connection, to me, is having a little piece of your own personal heaven to go to or experience any time you want.

Craig

A few weeks into the class, we did the exercises on sending energy to different energy centers in each other. After the class we went back to a friend's house as a group for the night. We proceeded to try to send energy to each other with various exercises. It was amazing to me how the more we tried, the more we noticed the connection. It almost felt like the area receiving the energy felt like it was being physically touched. It was very amazing and exciting how we could connect energetically with each other.

Mary

For me there is a knowing in my gut that I am supposed to pay attention to any person I feel connected to. They have something to share with me or I with them. When I feel a strong energetic connection, I usually find some way to be around this person, to be friends, or to be connected work associates. If I do not feel any energy around a relationship, I usually do not spend time with it. I have learned to pay attention to my feelings and to connect to those people, places, or things that have the most positive energy for me.

For You

We encourage you to explore the following questions for yourself to search for your own way of integrating spirituality into your life.

- Do you feel energetic connections to people?

- Is there some place that makes you feel especially safe or good?

- Do you admit to yourself that energetic connections affect you?

- How often are you aware of the energy of others?

- Do you know you are allowed to leave when the energy is not right for you?

- Do you follow your heart when the energy in a situation is not right for you?

When you are emotionally upset, what do you do to calm down?

Meg

When I'm upset, I take myself into the center of the thing that is upsetting me. I imagine sending little beads of light to that upsetting thing until it slowly dissipates and is finally gone. It also helps to associate things with color. If the upsetting emotion can be compared with the color blue, then I imagine sending gold light towards it to brighten it up some. Or if I'm raging and associating my rage with the color red, I send blue light towards it to calm it down. Colors play a big part in emotions. That's why often, when I'm upset, I paint or color until I get all of that emotion out.

Craig

When I'm upset, it helps me to calm down if I go outside. I go where there are no people and I stop and look at nature. I close my eyes, take a deep breath, and just feel the positive energy that nature has to provide. This is a very calming experience which has saved me from being over stressed or angry many times.

Brian

There are many things I do when emotionally upset to calm myself down. I usually try to take some deep breaths, because breathing is important to get me centered. Then I think about what is bothering me. I usually ask myself why is this upsetting me? Are there issues of self-worth? Self-confidence? Am I insecure? I always make sure that what I am upset about is worthwhile. If it is something that is insignificant, I do what I can to forget about it. If what I am feeling is some sort of pain or sadness or anything like that, I make sure to **feel** it. I let myself feel my emotions. This could take a lot of crying or a little silence, but I let the emotions serve their purpose no matter what. Lastly I step as boldly as possible into a decision. Sometimes it means I have to confront someone or do something else that is hard for me. I try to make the right decision and stick to it. I kiss the experience goodbye, having served its purpose, and, then, I move on.

Todd

The best way I have found to get through the toughest times emotionally in my life has been to step back from the situation and look at the big picture. Previous to my energetic awareness I would use this technique to show the insignificance of whatever was bothering me at the time. I would take comfort in the idea that whatever it was didn't really matter as you look at the bigger picture. This worked well for me and still does, but when I use higher awareness to look at the big picture energetically, it is even more comforting. When I can step back and look at the energy of whatever is bothering me, it is almost always clear what I need to do. This energy skill helps me everyday to see things in a better way.

Chris

I've had lots of years to try and get this right... and I definitely am better at it than I used to be. If I get upset now, I know it's my fault. My fault, my choice, my plan. Even if someone else does something mean or degrading toward me, it is still "I" who makes the choice to be upset about it. Really, the behaviors of other people and the actions of the world are out of my control. What is in my control is how I enjoy my life or choose not to. I always find myself asking the question: do I want to let this bother me or not? Do I want to feel upset about something? Most often the answer is no. So, to calm down, I try to: remove myself from the situation, honor the upset, take responsibility for my own feelings, and look to how it mirrors the state of my own soul. What are my upset feelings trying to tell me about myself?

Mary

I have battled with my emotions most of my life. I have tried to control them, stifle them or run away from them. But now, I try to take time to feel and understand what I am experiencing. If I get very upset, I will make a point to meditate and get into a higher state of consciousness. These higher states can help me view my situation differently. I can see what is really the source of my upset. We have all been in the habit of blaming others for our anger, fear, or unhappiness. But I have learned that negative self feelings or inner judgments or being the self critic is usually the source of my emotional upset. Meditating helps me remember that I have a soul and connects me with the peace always available in the higher energies. I can view my emotions as energy and send light to change this energy.

For You

The following questions will help you explore how you may calm yourself down.

- How do you know when you are upset?

- What kinds of places, activities, or people calm you down?

- Do you feel you need to stay in your upset?

- Do you like being emotionally upset? At any level?

- How can your higher self help you with your emotions?

How has sensing energy helped you deal with your romantic relationships?

Brian

My energy skills have helped immensely in this area. First, I can sense moods and problems quicker and better than before. When problems do arise, I try to sense the energy of the situation. I recently had an impulse to smudge my girlfriend and so I followed it. It turned out really well. She liked the experience a lot and so did I. Using my awareness of energy has made it easier to connect to a person in a romantic relationship. Looking deep into her eyes is different for me than it used to be, and I also do it a lot more often.

Probably the biggest help energy skills have given me in these relationships is letting go of control dramas. I believe that control dramas are most present in romantic relationships. It makes a big difference for me to stay in my own power without playing games. It makes things easier to work out because we can cut through the crap and get straight to the issue. Problems are usually caused by a single emotion and I am better able to see that now. I also try to make sure that there is an equal energy exchange between us. If that is not the case, I try to change the imbalance or look for someone with whom I can have that occur.

Todd

It has been my experience that most of the problems caused in romantic relationships comes from a need by one partner or the other that is not being filled. This often leads to an energetic struggle between a couple where both partners feel as if their needs are not being met. Being able to sense energy allows me to stop stealing energy before it starts. The best portions of my romantic relationships have been times where the two of us didn't need one another for energy. We simply enjoyed the energy of being together. The energy of the universe is so boundless that it fills me with hope. I have also found that when I can sense energy and be in a positive energy state, the effects on my partner are extremely positive, too.

Meg

Certain people send out certain energies. When I notice energies that appeal to me are coming from a person, I become attracted to them. It's the same with energies that don't appeal to me. If I sense a person is giving off pessimistic, rude, or violent energies, I choose not to get romantically involved with them. There were times when I felt a tingling, like someone staring at me, and have turned around to find someone staring at me. I sensed their energy. You can easily find energy in a smile, glare, or frown.

Chris

Relationships still demand work and are sources of wonderful delight and worrisome fear for me. At another level, it makes everything so much better. I got divorced a few years ago and I discovered that most of my attitudes about myself, my wife, my marriage, my place in life, my way of behaving, my goals, my achievements, heck, my totality, had been defined by other people, not by my own careful listening to my own energy. Wow, what a wake up call when I started listening! Now I enter relationships knowing my full responsibility for myself and permitting my loved one to be also fully responsible for herself. Sometimes that is really scary and worrisome. But the highs I can get now, in the midst of a relationship where both sides take care of their own stuff, are so much clearer, cleaner, and higher than ever before, it doesn't feel like the same kind of relationship at all. One fearful thing I had to face was whether or not there were any women with this higher view of relationships. There are many! It's just that, from where I was, I couldn't see or appreciate them!

For You

These questions can help you clarify for yourself how to have more loving relationships in your life.

- How does the energy of love improve your life?

- Can you feel the energy of your lover better than you can the energy of other people?

- Do you trust your energetic feelings about your boyfriend or girlfriend?

- How much of your self are you willing to give up to please your partner? What are the energetic implications of doing this?

- How often does your partner drain your energy?

- Do you look to your partner to make you feel worth loving?

How have you changed a bad situation into a good one by using energy and light?

Craig

Often when I have to audition for shows, I get very nervous. Although it usually isn't positive, being nervous creates a lot of energy. If I concentrate on changing that negative nervous energy into something positive and supportive, it not only helps with the nervousness but is actually works for me and helps make my performance better.

Meg

Bad situations, for me, are brought on by stress of some sort. "Oh no! I have an exam I forgot about!" or "So much to do, so little time," or "I have too many problems to solve and all at once!" It's almost funny to see people get so overwhelmed. And everything can be solved so easily if you just know how to center yourself. That is the beginning of turning a situation around. I start by closing my eyes and imagining the short time I have to complete something expanding on a vast plane. Then, instead of imagining getting everything done the fastest and most efficient way, I imagine completing one task slowly and exactly the way I want to complete it. Then I open my eyes and start with the first task that comes to mind. I don't think about any others until I have completed it. Your sub-conscious is on your side and if you only spend a little time connecting with it, you'll find the shortcut through bad situations.

Chris

Lighten up, lighten up, **lighten up**! That is one thing I have learned to do, at least a little, through all of this energy work. It was so easy, before, to take myself and my small little view of the world as **so important**! It was like, if the world didn't run according to my very detailed yet accommodating perspective, then something was wrong and I was upset. I've never had a time where I laugh at myself as much as I do now. It's been said before – you are not your body, you are not your thoughts, you are not your emotions, you are not your mind, you are much bigger and grander and more beautiful than all of that. The important part for me was to realize that **I am not my emotions**! I was stuck there for a long time and, now, even in the middle of a bad situation with negative emotions fully engaged, it will come to me that I am more than that feeling of negative emotion. And I lighten up. And things get better.

Mary

Learning to meditate and getting out of my small self and into my soul self has changed every part of my life. When something bad was happening I used to suffer, I felt I had no power to change a bad situation. I did not understand that it was my feelings and attitude about the event that made me suffer, not the event. As a social worker, I know that in every life bad things will happen. No one's life is free of pain, disappointment, and loss. But, do you have to live in pain for a long time? The answer is no! The way I change a bad situation into a good situation is by working on releasing the negative energy of this situation from my energy field. The way I do this is through meditation. I know that by bringing in the higher light and the energy of the higher wisdom will show me how to change a negative into a positive. I also now understand that some negative events are my lessons in life. I need to look at negativity, not run away from it. There is always something to learn and a higher interpretation of bad events. It's up to me to find the meaning, add light, and transform the negative into positive. This is what keeps the joy flowing in my life.

For You

These questions will focus your attention on the ways you can change a bad situation into a good one. Though it may be a long time before you really believe, you can change anything.

- Can positive energy change a bad situation?

- Can you put loving energy into your problems without feeling drained?

- Can you think of a way to change the negative energy of a problem you have by working with spiritual energy?

- What is the difference between putting loving energy into a bad situation and avoiding a bad situation?

- How easy or hard is it for you, energetically, to let go of negative feelings about a situation?

If you could change something within yourself, what would you change?

Todd

I would change my life so that I never worried. My life, often times, seems overwhelmed with worry about money, school, relationships, etc. The worst thing about worry is that it gets me nowhere. I have never changed things for the better by worrying about them. So why do I worry? I worry because I am not exactly the person I want to be yet. Meditation and energy skills have helped me to let go of many of my everyday worries by guiding me into actions that release my worries about things. I wish it were easy to let go of my worry, but it never has been. This book offers skills and techniques that have been very helpful to me at times when I am really down about something. Energetic awareness offers such hope for me because of its power to guide me in the direction I am meant to go (without worry! Well, sometimes, anyway).

Meg

I would try and harness certain energies I know I already have but just cannot use for some reason or another. Part of the reason I cannot use these certain energies is skepticism. Everyone has a bit of skepticism about something or other in his or her life. If we could just get rid of it, I believe it would better our lives.

Craig

If I could change something energetically speaking, it would be that everybody could be more aware of their energetic surroundings and learn how to take advantage of energy in a positive way.

Mary

I would let go of worrying. I worry when I cannot control a situation or a relationship in my life. And, I know logically I have no power to control others, I only have the power to control myself. Yet, I worry . It is a pattern of negative thinking within me that I continue to work on changing. When I **trust** or I am **trusting**, I do not worry. Letting go of worry for me is a matter of trusting myself, trusting the Universe, trusting my soul to guide me, and trusting that all things in my life have a purpose. Trust is peace and love. Worry is fear and doubt. I must keep choosing trust to have a life of joy.

Chris

The one thing that I need to change and am changing is my belief in expectations. I'm a very intellectual person, heck, I'm a college professor. So I've spent my life building up all these complex models about the universe, psychology, God, religion, life, and other people. Every model says the same thing: **here is what to expect.** And I can get agitated when the world doesn't operate according to schedule.

I know that I think we need understanding to work together in this world, but I don't know that my thinking is right. What if we let the synchronicity of life direct much of what we do? What if we spend time planning but then feel no investment in the plan and feel free to toss it away. Here is the point: I feel pain and fear mostly when the world doesn't act according to my expectations. I believe my task is **not** to try to improve my models but to discard my emotional attachment to these expectations and just accept that "no doubt, the universe is unfolding as it should" (from the poem Desiderata). Acceptance.

For You

These questions are meant to help you explore how to change things on the energy level. It always takes a great deal of awareness and courage to change yourself.

- What do you want to change about yourself or your life?

- How could you align the body, emotions, mind, and spirit to make these changes?

- Are you afraid of making changes?

- What does your soul want for you?

- Are you the most important person in your life?

- In what ways do you think negatively about yourself? Is that right? Do you think of others that way? Should you think of yourself negatively?

But how do you heal yourself when something really terrible happens?

Forgiveness

Both Chris and Mary wanted to answer this question because it is a very important aspect of energy work and healing the self. We want you to reach your highest potential. To do that, you will need to release the negative energy of events and resentments when bad things happen. Part of the path of becoming a Master is to learn how to forgive and let go. It is the only way to heal negativity and be free. When you are free you can live as your soul.

Chris

I know a dear woman who was severely abused as a child, abused to a point that suicide seemed like the answer even at the age of seven. You probably know someone like this but may not yet have found out the truth.

While working in a personal growth seminar with this woman, I saw one of the other male participants leave the building enraged. He had heard the woman's story. He had felt her great grief. He stormed around the area muttering about wanting to kill the abuser.

Three things became clear to me.

My tears of sadness flowed easily for the abused woman. Her pain was still there below the surface, locked in the abused child within. The inhumanity that one person can show another is staggering. It is also sad that these events that happened decades ago still had such a profound effect on her current reality. It is her own memory of the hurt that remains. It is her own hanging on to this painful energy that keeps those moments of abuse alive.

My tears of sadness flowed for the enraged man. He was taking on the energy of anger for an event that occurred decades ago. He was making a conscious choice to disrupt the peace in his life because of an ancient hurt he could not touch or affect. He took on the painful energy of another.

Finally, my tears of sadness even flowed for the long ago abuser. The abuser was, once upon a time, a young child, with an innocent view of life, looking forward to each day with joy and anticipation. Something was done to this child to make him or her become an abuser. The details will remain unknown forever. But the chain of hurtful behavior started long before this abuse was committed.

Forgiveness. Nothing can be more important to you. Forgive yourself. Forgive the abusers in your life. Forgive everyone that you feel has wronged you.

Forgiveness is the process of you unhooking your own life's energy from your past. If you cannot disconnect from your past and become detached from it, your future will always be constrained due to your limited current energy. The practice that can help you forgive is to first accept all the emotions of sadness or terror or rage that have coursed through you because of events in your life. Sit in them. Feel them so that you do not become them. Eventually, you will decide. You will come to know that the only thing that sitting in anger and pity does is make you angry and pitiful. Why spend your life force energy in this way? Your energy and higher potential need not stay locked in the hurts of the past.

We will bring peace into this world only when we start to forgive each other of everything, no matter how deep the hurt or how depraved the behavior. If you do not forgive, you hurt yourself.

Mary

Having compassion for your fellow human beings is a way to learn how to have compassion for yourself. Forgiveness, compassion, and love are all part of the same higher energy flow. When we hang on to the energy of resentment and old hurts, we restrict the flow of love in our own life. There is nothing more uplifting and beautiful than experiencing the freedom of living in the present. Being able at any moment to love and express yourself freely. This cannot happen if you hang onto the energy of the past.

Being able to forgive the worst sin that has ever happened to you is a very high state of being. It is something that may have to be worked on for a while before you can truly be free. Carrying around the energy of hate, anger, or loathing is like carrying heavy chains of energy. These chains keep you at a lower level energetically. They prevent you from rising into the light. They will keep you from being all you can be. We can only fully and completely love ourselves when we let go of the chains of negative energy. When we release others to their own higher path, we, in turn, will be released to live our own highest path.

There is much higher light in the energy of freedom. Being free is an enlightened state. Give yourself the gift of energetic freedom. Let go and live in the light.

Conclusion

Since we completed our original group, Chris, Mary, Todd, Brian, Meg, and Craig have continued to meet periodically. We have meditated and explored energies together. We had some groups at Michigan State University and introduced other young people to this work. Along the way, we have continued to deepen our own energetic connection to each other and to our souls. We have also experienced stronger connections to our "guides" and the Higher Communities of Light. When we meditate together, we can often sense the presence of other souls or great beings of light with us.

Each one of these young people has been willing to open themselves to new thoughts, new ideas, and spiritual growth. They have all gained confidence in connecting the body, mind, and spirit, coming to a new understanding of their own greater self.

Using energy in your life means taking on a new perspective. You are a soul having a human experience. Wisdom, peace, and higher guidance, is already there within your soul's energy. You will need to learn new skills of listening and exploring to become effective at using spiritual energies in your life. Growing beyond your personality self and experiencing your higher potential is a process. When you decide to be more aware of your spirit self, it will unfold step by step.

What would your life be like if you sent light rather than aggression to your conflicts? What would your relationships be like if you let go of the power struggles? What would the world be like if all people consulted with their higher self before making business or governmental decisions? In our groups we posed these and other questions to have all of us look at life from a higher perspective. When you join together and explore spiritual energies and search for your truth, something extraordinary happens; your soul speaks to your heart and you uncover the true meaning of your life.

We had fun together. It has been a powerful bonding experience and we, the authors, believe our group will be connected for this lifetime and beyond. These youth have shown us that young people are ready to learn about spiritual energies. If it is part of their higher path, they are ready to grow to enlightenment in this new age. All four of the Young Old Masters are off in different directions, pursuing their own destiny. We said goodbye to each other in a physical sense, but we know that we can connect on the inner planes anytime. Our spirits have no boundaries; therefore, time and space cannot separate us.

We send you, the reader, a wave of love and our sincere support in discovering your own spiritual connections. Believe in yourself and the power of your soul to transform your life. Believe in the power of many souls to transform the world with light. Create your own spiritual awareness group and explore the higher dimensions together. Remember, you too, are a Master.

Principled Living, Our Hope for You

This is the end of the book. Time for you to stop listening to someone else and start listening to yourself. Time for you to begin to know your truth in life. It is time for you to feel the hope available when you align your body, emotions, mind, and spirit with the spiritual forces that can guide you toward an enlightened life.

We conclude with the following principles that seem to be true no matter who you are:

Principle: *You Create Your Reality.*

This is difficult to understand and accept because we think others have control over our lives. The more you become aligned with this truth, the more you will be able to create the kind of life your really want. Even when bad things happen, you have the choice to create peace for yourself. Your soul wants you to know and believe you are powerful. You and your higher self, in partnership with the divine will, create your life.

Principle: *You Create Your Reality With the Assistance of the Divine.*

You will be blocked energetically when you are moving against your higher self. When you experience pain, when doors are closing, when life isn't working, you are being asked by the Divine mind, the higher intelligence, to change your path. Remember to notice if the universe is supporting your desires. Does it feel like you are being led toward your highest path? When your life is flowing easily, you are aligned with the Divine plan for you.

Principle: *You Can Manifest Your Desires.*

Your dreams, hopes, and desires are part of the Divine plan for your life. This is what your soul wants for you too. Remember the universe is perfect. It will bring you your desires in the HIGHEST way. Let go of your expectations and allow the higher flow to bring you your destiny as it unfolds, in a perfect way, in accordance with Divine timing.

Principle: *You Must Love Yourself First.*

To have all the joy and love you would ever want begins with yourself. If you do not have an inner source of love available, no one can ever give you enough loving energy to satisfy your need for love. Our soul's essence is the energy of love. There is no shortage of energy and love available from your soul. Give yourself a hug and love and appreciate you. Loving and honoring yourself will do more for healing the planet than anything else. It will also do more for bringing you an abundance of true happiness and loving relationships.

Principle: *We are not Separate.*

Even though we have our own path and our own journey to experience here on earth, as beings of energy we are connected to each other, to animals, to plants, to Mother Earth, herself. An enlightened person knows that if even the least person among us is hungry, in some manner you are hungry too. If the least person among us is hurt or in pain, at some level we are all hurt and in pain. As more people align with the vibration of love, more love is available for all.

Principle: *You, too, Are a Master.*

You are a great soul. You have a purpose here on earth. You are wise. You are capable of great things. Believe in yourself and allow the Master that you are to evolve and grow into the light of your highest potential.

THE BEGINNING

CHAPTER 9 🌀 Creating a Better Life

OME Press will be releasing meditation tapes that complement the energy exercises in this book later in 1998. Each tape has been channeled to help address the energy issues of a particular chapter. Contact us at OME Press if you are interested.

The whole point of this book is to give you hope for a fulfilling life. Now you *know* you can look at things differently. If you are willing to integrate spirit into your life, we, as a new age begins, are opening up ways to reach our highest potential. Through our experiences, we now know we can change our lives. Human life is a journey to move us higher, not lower. Hope is an energy that brings with it possibilities of evolving into our highest potential. You know you have a fulfilling life when you are filled with love and fun and joy. This is our hope for you.

As you have begun to watch your energy skills improve, we know the feeling of hope that begins to arise deep within your heart. Your soul showers you with love and joy as you are proceeding down the only important journey in your life, the journey to discover who you are and to learn to be that person in every moment of every day. Your light, your joy, your passion for this new life can be increased every day... if you just keep working at it. This last chapter of the book is a pointer to other sources of information, other activities, and other views on living your life fully and rightly. Of course, it isn't exhaustive and complete. There are just too many different sources available now as the world moves toward a period of enlightenment. But consider looking into each of these, as we are only including those works that have been meaningful to some member of our group.

Other Readings

The number of books that can help you grow and heal are many. We have listed here just a few of the books that have been especially powerful for us in our work. New ones are created almost daily as the energies of light and healing continue to bathe the earth. Enjoy them.

Some of the works listed here are from channels. There is some confusion about what a channel is, and we'd just like to make a short comment. When a person channels, they go within and connect to the divine light. Sometimes the connection to that light is a connection to their own soul. At other times, higher beings come to speak through the person. Virtually all religions of the world have some words that speak of higher connection, for example, Christianity talks of angels, archangels, seraphims, and the like.

The bottom line is that none of the works described here demand that you have a particular religious conviction. Instead of worrying about how the information was transmitted to this realm, ask yourself what the information does for you. There have been prophets and seers in all religions since the beginning of time. We firmly believe that God continues to speak to us in this world. He uses each one of us, in greater and lesser ways, to spread the message of love.

The works of Sanaya Roman and Duane Packer

Orin is an energy channeled by Sanaya Roman while DaBen is an energy channeled by Duane Packer. These particular channels have had a tremendous impact on Mary and Chris. Mary and Chris are both teachers of Orin and DaBen's "Light Body" meditation technique; they originally met in a seminar put on by Sanaya and Duane.

Several books and many cassette tapes are available through their work. Some of the more important books are:

Roman, S. (1986) *Living With Joy: Keys to Personal Power and Spiritual Transformation*, Tiburon, CA: H J Kramer Inc. ISBN 0-915811-09-X.

Roman, S. (1986) *Personal Power Through Awareness: A Guidebook for Sensitive People*, Tiburon, CA: H J Kramer Inc.

Roman, S. (1989) *Spiritual Growth: Being Your Higher Self*, Tiburon, CA: H J Kramer Inc. ISBN 0-915811-12-X.

Roman, S. & Packer D. (1989) *Opening to Channel: How to Connect with Your Guide*, Tiburon, CA: H J Kramer Inc.

Roman, S. & Packer D. (1988) *Creating Money: Keys to Abundance*, Tiburon, CA: H J Kramer Inc.

Sanaya and Duane also offer many tape courses through their company LuminEssence, P.O. Box 1310, Medford, OR, 97501. Their telephone number is (541) 770-6700. Some of the important tape series are:

Awakening Your Light Body: A Course in Enlightenment This is a six volume cassette course with six two-sided cassettes in each volume. Conscientious study of the material takes between 6 to 12 months to complete. Light body teachers can be found throughout the world to aid in the teaching, though it can be done alone with just the tapes.

Living With Joy. Volume 1: Living with Joy, Volume 2: Taking a Quantum Leap.

Personal Power Through Awareness. Volume 1: Sensing Energy, Volume 2: Journey Into Light - Going Higher.

Spiritual Growth. Volume 1: Raising Your Vibration, Volume 2: Being Your Higher Self.

Becoming a World Server.

Opening to Channel, Improve Your Channeling, Advanced Channeling Skills.

Many other taped courses are available only to those people who have completed the Light Body course. Once the Light Body skills are completed, many realms of higher energy work are available for consideration.

The works of Neale Donald Walsch

Walsch was a man who chose to write letters to people when angry and inflamed as a means of dissipating destructive energy. One day he wrote an angry letter to God. As he wrote the letter, he asked God "What had I done to deserve a life of such continuing struggle?"

Then God took over his hand and wrote on the page "Do you really want an answer to all these questions or are you just venting?"

Hence began a conversation between Walsch and God that has, at this date, spanned two books and will soon include a third.

Walsch, N.D. (1997) *Conversations with God: an Uncommon Dialog - Book 1*, Charlottesville, VA: Hampton Roads Publishing Company, Inc. ISBN 1-57174-025-2.

Walsch, N.D. (1997) *Conversations with God: an Uncommon Dialog - Book 2*, Charlottesville, VA: Hampton Roads Publishing Company, Inc. ISBN 1-57174-056-2.

The works of James Redfield

James Redfield's book, The Celestine Prophecy is, to some degree, responsible for the creation of this book. It was a group of teenage kids wanting to discuss the ideas in this book that led to the young persons seminar, that led to the astounding mastery of young people being revealed to Chris and Mary, that led to the writing of this book.

Redfield, J. (1993) *The Celestine Prophecy: An Adventure*, New York: Warner Books, Inc. ISBN 0-446-51862-X.

Redfield, J. & Adrienne, C. (1995) *The Celestine Prophecy: An Experiential Guide*, New York: Warner Books, Inc. ISBN 0-446-67122-3.

Redfield, J. (1996) *The Tenth Insight: Holding the Vision*, New York: Warner Books, Inc. ISBN 0-446-51908-1.

Redfield, J. & Adrienne, C. (1996) *The Tenth Insight: Holding the Vision: An Experiential Guide*, New York: Warner Books, Inc. ISBN 0-446-67299-8.

The works of Helen Schucman and William Thetford

Helen Schucman was a Professor of Medical Psychology at Columbia University's College of Physicians and Surgeons in New York City. She had a confrontation with her department head, William Thetford who, in disgust at the angry and aggressive feelings in his department, said "there must be another way." As if on cue, Helen started having vivid dreams and hearing voices in her head. She described it in the following words

> "the Voice. It made no sound, but seemed to be giving me a kind of rapid, inner dictation which I took down in a shorthand notebook. The writing was never automatic. It could be interrupted at any time and later picked up again. It made me very uncomfortable, but it never seriously occurred to me to stop."

The first words she wrote were "This is a course in miracles." Indeed, that is the name of the book created by their collaboration: *A Course in Miracles*. It is a set of three books – a text, a workbook for students, and a manual for teachers that took over 12 years to complete. The book is probably the most profound work ever written, even when compared to the bible. The book supports God and Christ in a way that is completely consistent with the bible, but not necessarily consistent with how any particular church interprets the bible. The most astounding thing about the work is that, from beginning to end, over 1200 pages, there are no self contradictions. The work never says one thing on one page and a contradictory thing somewhere else in the book. Reading it makes one believe that it was divinely inspired.

The work started by *A Course in Miracles* is continued by the Foundation for Inner Peace in Glen Ellen, California.

Foundation for Inner Peace. (1975, 1985, 1992). *A Course in Miracles*. Glen Ellen, CA: Foundation for Inner Peace. ISBN 0-0606388-8-1.

The works of Jane Roberts and Robert Butts

No doubt, the best way to introduce Seth is through the words of Jane Roberts, the woman who brought him to the world.

"My psychic initiation really began one evening in September, 1963, however, as I saw writing poetry. Suddenly my consciousness left my body, and my mind was barraged by ideas that were astonishing and new to me at the time. On return to my body, I discovered that my hands had produced an automatic script, explaining many of the concepts that I'd been given. ...Not long after, however, I felt impelled to say the words aloud, and within a month I was speaking for Seth while in a trance state. ...

Since then, Seth has delivered a continuing manuscript that now totals over six thousand typewritten pages. We call it the Seth material..."

The material produce by Seth is wonderful. It is warm and inviting, saturated with love and wisdom. As is true for so much of the material be channeled throughout the world, it does not contradict any religious perspective but seems to support all people's search for the divine in their lives.

Roberts, J. (1995), Notes by Robert F. Butts, *The Individual and the Nature of Mass Events*, San Rafael, CA: Amber-Allen Publishing, Inc. ISBN 1-878424-21-1.

Roberts, J. (1995), Notes by Robert F. Butts, *The Magical Approach: Seth Speaks About the Art of Creative Living*, San Rafael, CA: Amber-Allen Publishing, Inc. ISBN 1-878424-09-2.

Roberts, J. (1994), Notes by Robert F. Butts, *The Nature of Personal Reality: Specific, Practical Techniques for Solving Everyday Problems and Enriching the Life You Know*, San Rafael, CA: Amber-Allen Publishing, Inc. ISBN 1-878424-06-8.

Roberts, J. (1995), Notes by Robert F. Butts, *The Nature of the Psyche: Its Human Expression*, San Rafael, CA: Amber-Allen Publishing, Inc. ISBN 1-878424-22-X.

Roberts, J. (1995). *The Oversoul Seven Trilogy*, San Rafael, CA: Amber-Allen Publishing, Inc. ISBN 1-878424-17-3.

Roberts, J. (1996). Notes by Robert F. Butts, *The "Unkown" Reality: Volume One*, San Rafael, CA: Amber-Allen Publishing, Inc. ISBN 1-878424-25-4.

The works of Pat Rodegast and Judith Stanton

Pat Rodegast had an experience that is becoming not uncommon throughout the world, another feeling that another being is present to the inner self. In her own words in the book *Emmanuel's Book* she says:

"During my TM meditations, I became distracted by inner visions, which continued despite my efforts to suppress them. I finally decided to allow these visions their space. ... The first time I saw Emmanuel, some two years after the initial visual breakthrough, he appeared, as he stil oes, as a being of golden light. ... So I offer you my dearest, wisest, sweetest, funniest, Absolute friend Emmanuel."

The true joy in reading the works of Emmanuel is that Emmanuel speaks as a poet. Not with strict rhyme or meter, but with that attention to cadence and nuance of words that is missing in ordinary prose. Many of the selections in any of the books can bring tears to your eyes, tears of warmth, and joy, and love.

Rodegast, P. & J. Stanton. (1985). *Emmanuel's Book: A Manual for Living Comfortably in the Cosmos*, New York: Bantam Books. ISBN 0-553-34387-4.

Rodegast, P. & J. Stanton. (1989). *Emmanuel's Book II: The Choice for Love*, New York: Bantam Books. ISBN 0-553-34750-0.

Rodegast, P. & J. Stanton. (1994). *Emmanuel's Book III: What is an Angel Doing Here?*, New York: Bantam Books. ISBN 0-553-37412-5.

The works of Edgar Cayce

Edgar Cayce is probably the best known psychic in American history. The Association for Research and Enlightenment, Inc. in Virginia is a non-profit organization dedicated to educating people about the information and philosophy contained in Cayce's work.

The stories about Cayce are astounding and legion and far too numerous and complex to recount here. From an early age, he would go into a sleep state and come back knowing things. He had trouble in school as a young child until he realized that he could go to sleep thinking about the material and awake with a photographic memory of an entire book. He gave medical readings for people around the country for decades, in which he would sleep for a short time and awaken with full knowledge about a patient's problem and, if possible, appropriate methods for treatment. He did all this while remaining a most devout Christian. Though he did not understand it, he knew his readings were a gift from God. All readings that Cayce ever did have been collected on a CD available from the ARE. Just consider one book to introduce yourself to this amazing man.

Sugrue, Thomas. (1942, 1973). *There is a River: The Story of Edgar Cayce*. Virginia Beach, VA: A.R.E.® Press. ISBN 87604-235-3.

The works of Carolyn Myss

Carolyn Myss (pronounced "mace") is a medical intuitive. Her own words describe her movement into this ability.

"... I gradually recognized that my perceptual abilities had expanded considerably. For instance, a friend would mention that someone he knew was not feeling well, and an insight into the cause of the problem would pop into my head, I was uncannily accurate,...I could not figure out how I was getting these impressions. They were, and still are, like impersonal daydreams that start to flow as soon as I receive a person's permission, name, and age."

Perhaps the most interesting comment she makes in her book is the following:

"No dramatic 'first event' ushered my intuitive abilities into my life. They simply woke up inside me, easily, naturally, as if they had always been there, awaiting the appropriate time to emerge."

How might the same be true for you?

Myss, Caroline. (1996). *Anatomy of the Spirit: The Seven Stages of Power and Healing*. New York: Harmony Books. ISBN 0-517-70391-2.

Divination tools

Have you ever wondered what movie you wanted to see? Maybe this one, maybe that one? Then, unable to decide, you pull out a coin and give it a flip. You'll go to the first movie if a head comes up, and go to the other if it is a tail. At some level, you're just having fun. At another level, you're putting your faith into the universe that it will pick the right one for you. Trusting in the universe is not a stupid thing to do... after all it did work to create you and have you standing there wondering which movie to see.

We are including this section on divination tools so that you can have some fun. Please, a divination tool is not something by which you should run your life. If you find yourself running to a tool at every drop of the hat, you need to get a grip and remember that you are in charge of your existence. Nonetheless, a divination tool can be a way to help you focus your own thinking. Going quiet inside yourself, finding a question for which you wish to have some insight, shuffling a deck of cards and drawing whichever one seems right is an easy task. When you look at the card you've drawn and open your heart to the messages that come forth, it helps you think, points to lacks in your awareness, suggests alternatives not apparent to you.

So we suggest that you not get overly concerned with the idea of divining your truth (divining comes from the word "divine"). Just keep thinking, keep paying attention, keep living, in any way that sharpens your focus on why you are here and what you are here to achieve.

Sams, J. & Carson, D. (1988). *Medicine Cards: The Discovery of Power Through the Ways of Animals.* Santa Fe: New

Mexico: Bear & Company. ISBN 0-939680-53-X.

Deer, Chief Archie Fire Lame, & Sarkis, Helene. (1994). *Lakota Sweat Lodge: Spiritual Teachings of the Sioux.* Rochester, Vermont: Destiny Books. ISBN 0-89281-456-X.

Osho International Foundation. (1994). *Osho Zen Tarot: The Transcendental Game of Zen.* New York: St. Martin's Press. ISBN 0-312-11733-7.

Blum, R. H. (1993). *The Book of Runes: A Handbook for the Use of an Ancient Oracle: The Viking Runes.* New York: St. Martin's Press. ISBN 0-312-09758-1.

Music

Music is one of the most powerful ways in which we can affect our internal emotional lives. The youth of any era sound forth with a style of musical expression unique to themselves and their energy. As a new era of light continues on this planet, some varieties of music seem to clearly support the emotional mind set that makes higher energies accessible. Some of our favorites, among many, many others, are described below.

The works of Stephen Halpern

Stephen Halpern has created powerful new age music for many years. Fortunately his work is available in every music store you can find. Just ask for him by name and take home a powerful and loving musical experience.

The works of Michael Hammer

Michael Hammer's works have become staples to people involved in Orin and DaBen's meditation as he provides much of the musical background for their work. His works can be ordered through LuminEssence, P.O. Box 1310, Medford, OR, 97501. Their telephone number is (541) 770-6700.

The works of Wild Roses: Cinde Borup and Beth Pederson

Though they do not have many CD's available at the current time, the gentleness of their music is profound. At last check they had produced two wonderful CDs together. Listen to them both!

Wild Roses. (1994). *Voices on the Wind*. Sandpoint, ID: High Moon Music.

Wild Roses. (1994). *Northern Lights*. Sandpoint, ID: High Moon Music.

The Music Labels of Windham Hills and Narada

Music labels make a choice about the type of music they will produce. The two separate labels of Windham Hills and Narada have a commitment to make some of the best new age music around. To get started in their collection, they each produce sampler albums at various times that includes the best songs from across the many artists they record.

Organizations

The works of Bill Cauth

In conversations with Bill Cauth, he said that one of the motivators of his life's work was a worry that the many over-testosteroned men in the world might well blow us all to kingdom come in a nuclear war. He has focussed his work on helping men be true men for many years. He is one of the co-founders of the New Warrior movement for men.

New Warrior Network

A man's introduction to New Warrior work begins with an initiation weekend, 48 hours, from Friday night to Sunday afternoon. The precise details of this weekend are not discussed because much of the powerful effect of the weekend on a man comes as a result of the unknown trials that face him during the experience. The weekend is *not* about paintball guns in the woods. That would be the old view of a warrior. The weekend *is* about the extreme challenges a man must face to see himself for who he is, to accept that current self, and to move to ever improve upon who he is and how he treats others. Chris, Brian and Todd have all been through the New Warrior weekend and the weeks of follow-on work that cements the changes in a man.

There is only one more comment that needs to be said. One week after the weekend adventure is a graduation ceremony. Many of the men on the weekend are married or in a deeply committed romantic relationship. It is common for the wives or significant others of these men to stand and honor these men. They have seen a difference in who they are related to after only one short week.

The Woman Within

The Woman Within weekend was created in response to the women wanting a similar experience for themselves. Since women come into their lives with different social backgrounds and life experiences than men do, they have different needs and the weekend is adjusted in important ways. At the very least, the women's weekend is less spartan than the men's. But it is no less transformational.

If you have trouble locating either the New Warrior Network or Women Within, please contact us to help you find them.

Twelve Step Programs

Many people's lives have been saved, literally saved, by participating in twelve step programs like Alcoholics Anonymous (AA), Narcotics Anonymous (NA), Alanon (for families of addicts). This is great work for understanding and healing yourself and taking personal responsibility for you life, especially for people recovering from addictions.

The twelve steps contained in the AA Big Book are listed below. Though they are focussed on alcohol, there words can have meaning for any part of your life that had become addictive.

1. We admitted we were powerless over alcohol that our lives had become unmanageable.

2. Came to believe that a Power greater than ourselves could restore us to sanity.

3. Made a decision to turn our will and our lives over to the care of God as we understood Him.

4. Made a searching and fearless moral inventory of ourselves.

5. Admitted to God, to ourselves, and to another human being the exact nature of our wrongs.

6. Were entirely ready to have God remove all these defects of character.

7. Humbly asked Him to remove our shortcomings.

8. Made a list of all persons we had harmed, and became willing to make amends to them all.

9. Made direct amends to such people wherever possible, except when to do so would injure them or others.

10. Continued to take personal inventory and when we were wrong promptly admitted it.

11. Sought through prayer and meditation to improve our conscious contact with God as we understood Him, praying only for knowledge of His will for us and the power to carry that out.

12. Having had a spiritual awakening as the result of these steps, we tried to carry this message to alcoholics, and to practice these principles in all our affairs.

Support Groups

We are people who are born into and live in communities. Often support groups give us a community of people with a similar problem to work through. Also, support groups can be empowering.

The End

Creating a Better Life

The Young Old Masters

About the Authors

Mary Norris, MSW.

Mary Norris is an intuitive teacher and a skilled group facilitator. Mary feels that part of her purpose is to teach others energy and light skills. As a professional with many years of health care and community service background, she is available to teach meditation to your group or organization. Mary may be contacted through OME Press.

Chris Wagner, Ph.D.

Chris Wagner has diverse interests ranging from consulting for the auto industry, teaching computer science and engineering, teaching meditation classes and playing music. For Chris, spiritual work plays an ever growing role in his daily life. Part of his purpose in life is to spread joy through the world by seeking the truth – a lesson learned in New Warrior training. Chris may be contacted at OME Press or through Oakland University in Rochester, Michigan.

OME Press

Chris, Mary and OME Press are committed to the growth and enlightenment of young and the young of heart. We are open to supporting other authors of new-age materials.

OME Press
PO Box 278
Highland, Michigan 48357-0278
Phone: (248) 887-6216